Magdalena Droste

The Bauhaus

1919–1933

Reform and Avant

TASCHEN

HONGKONG KÖLN LONDON LOS ANGELES MADRID PARIS TOKYO

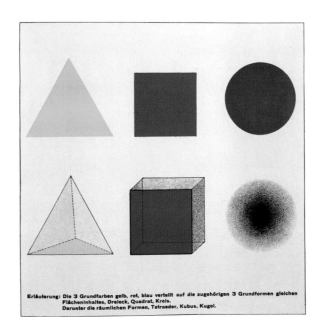

Erläuterung: Die 3 Grundfarben gelb, rot, blau verteilt auf die zugehörigen 3 Grundformen gleichen Flächeninhaltes, Dreieck, Quadrat, Kreis. Darunter die räumlichen Formen, Tetraeder, Kubus, Kugel.

© The Josef and Anni Albers Foundation/VG Bild-Kunst, Bonn 2006, of works by Josef Albers

© VG Bild-Kunst, Bonn 2006, of works by Karl Arnold, Herbert Bayer, Peter Behrens, Max Bill, Marianne Brandt, Lyonel Feininger, Walter Gropius, Johannes Itten, Paul Klee, Mies van der Rohe, Wassily Kandinsky, Lucia Moholy, László Moholy-Nagy, Gyula Pap, Joost Schmidt, Gunta Stölzl-Stadler, Wilhelm Wagenfeld, Andor Weininger

© 2006 TASCHEN GmbH
Hohenzollernring 53, D–50672 Köln
www.taschen.com

Edited by ▶ Peter Gössel, Bremen
Project management ▶ Swantje Schmidt, Bremen
Design and layout ▶ Gössel und Partner, Bremen
Text edited by ▶ Avinus, Berlin
Translation ▶ Maureen Roycroft Sommer, Bergisch Gladbach

Printed in Germany
ISBN 3-8228-3649-4

To stay informed about upcoming TASCHEN titles, please request our magazine at www.taschen.com/magazine or write to TASCHEN America, 6671 Sunset Boulevard, Suite 1508, USA-Los Angeles, CA 90028, contact-us@taschen.com, Fax: +1-323-463.4442. We will be happy to send you a free copy of our magazine which is filled with information about all of our books.

Contents

Prologue: Three Directors

To this day, the term Bauhaus has a novel ring to it. In common usage it marks the beginning of Modernism, triggering associations with basic forms (squares, triangles and circles) and primary colours (red, yellow and blue) as well as tubular steel furniture, white cubic architecture, and functionalism. Over the years, a mixture of fact and interpretation has obscured the history of this small German art school, which is what the Bauhaus was between 1919 and 1933. It now seems impervious to the results of detailed studies and new assessments. Nevertheless, the Bauhaus has become a phenomenon that every generation rediscovers for itself.

Contemporaries in the Weimar Republic tended to view the Bauhaus, after 1923, as a symbol of the drive towards rationalisation and modernisation in the home that spurned all superfluous creature comforts. At the same time it provoked the animosity of a sizeable, culturally conservative faction, often overlooked in conjunction with the "Golden Twenties". It seemed almost natural that the Bauhaus belonged on the left of the political spectrum. During the Third Reich (1933–1945) when People, Race, Homeland, and Classicism became the highest values of a perverted nation, the Bauhaus was disparaged as "culturally bolshevist", "internationalist" and "Jewish". Nevertheless, the Nazi regime made use of modern innovations. Most of the prominent members of the Bauhaus emigrated, and many of their Jewish relatives were murdered.

In East Germany, where the most important Bauhaus sites were located (Weimar and Dessau), the institution met with rejection after the war. Only in the late 1960s was it gradually subsumed as part of the country's "cultural heritage". In the Federal Republic and the United States, the Bauhaus was considered an essential aspect of Modernism well into the 1960s. Walter Gropius played a central role in this canonisation. Another piece of the mosaic was added with the establishment of the Bauhaus Archives in Darmstadt, later in Berlin.

The decades in which cultural politics mandated that the Bauhaus be viewed in a positive light slowly gave way to criticism and disparagement. In the United States the writer Tom Wolfe characterised the Bauhaus in his 1981 book *From Bauhaus to Our House* as a conspiracy to foster alienation in the country.

As a school, the Bauhaus had more facets than those conveyed by the "Bauhaus Myth", a term referring to the few basic ideas to which Gropius, its lifelong representative, reduced it. Gropius's successors Hannes Meyer (1928–1930) and Ludwig Mies van der Rohe (1930–1933) did not merely follow in his footsteps, they also became formidable opponents and rivals in the process of intellectually defining the Bauhaus. Both of them distanced themselves from Gropius and developed standpoints of their own, each inventing his own Bauhaus. Nevertheless, there was a degree of continuity, resulting above all from the Bauhaus's unwavering intention to institute anti-academic reform. These reforms were often related to avant-garde activities and sometimes took on an elitist character.

Left page:
Entrance to former Bauhaus after the last restoration in 2005 with doors painted again in the original shade of red.

7

Walter Gropius and His Path to the Bauhaus

Walter Gropius, benzene-fuelled locomotive, 1913/14
The locomotive was aerodynamically designed.

Today the emphasis is on the unique character of the Bauhaus, whereas in the years after its establishment in Weimar in 1919, Gropius was intent on integrating it into a network of other schools striving for reform. Both of these views have a degree of historical truth. As a reform project, the Bauhaus is deeply rooted in the cultural and intellectual tradition of late nineteenth century Wilhelminian historicism, a period when forces seeking innovative changes within the cultural context of the old authoritarian state began to stir.

After the establishment of the German Reich in 1871, a wave of modernisation transformed Germany from an agrarian to an industrial nation. It was flanked by population growth and the advent of mass culture. Among the reformers were Art Nouveau (*Jugendstil*) artists with centres in Darmstadt (Artists' Colony), Munich, and Dresden. They contributed to the spread of the British arts and crafts movement in Germany, a movement that actually opposed industrialisation. A number of the newly established schools were equipped with workshops. In retrospect, the Obrist-Debschitz Art School, established through private initiative in Munich in 1902, and the *Kunstgewerbeschule* (School of Arts and Crafts) in Weimar, under the direction of Henry van de Velde as of 1908, are now considered the most prominent. The Prussian state government recommended in 1904 that all of its art schools establish workshops.

The most important forum for debating reform was the *Deutscher Werkbund*, established in Munich in 1907 by architects, artists and entrepreneurs, an organisation in which private and state initiatives often formed alliances. The *Werkbund* sought to balance economic, artistic, and moral aims and to reconcile capitalism and culture. It was hoped that this reconciliation would be expressed in a new style.

The architect Walter Gropius (1883–1969) became a member of the *Werkbund* in 1910 and worked diligently, organising an exhibition on exemplary industrial architecture, editing the 1913 yearbook, *Die Kunst in Industrie und Handel* (Art in Industry and Trade), and giving lectures. He also became acquainted with branding—the development and presentation of brand name products such as it was at the time. Gropius's experience with the media at the Werkbund equipped him with many of the tools that he would need to head the Bauhaus effectively and manoeuvre into the public eye.

Before becoming involved with the Werkbund, Gropius had worked from June 1908 to March 1910 for Peter Behrens, one of Germany's most influential architects. Behrens, one of the founders of the Werkbund, became the "artistic advisor" to AEG (*Allgemeine Electricitäts Gesellschaft*), one of the world's largest manufacturers of electrical products, in 1907. He came to be called "Mr. Werkbund" (Julius Posener). As an employee in Behrens's office, Gropius witnessed the construction of the AEG turbine factory in 1908/09, a building with a façade framed by two impressive pylons and topped by a massive, sequentially angled gable, suggesting a radically simplified temple.

In 1911, Walter Gropius and his partner Adolf Meyer received their first independent commission for a factory building, the Fagus Factory in Alfeld near Hanover. The now world-famous building, featured in almost every book of architectural history, was not

Left page:
Photographic portrait of Walter Gropius, 1920

Peter Behrens, AEG Turbine Factory Berlin, 1909

Cartoon by Karl Arnold on a discussion in the Werkbund, 1914
Three ways to design a chair

completely ignored at the time, but Gropius's total avoidance of historicism was not fully recognised. With the "free-standing" glass corners and sparing use of brickwork, Gropius developed a novel artistic approach to building factories.

The Fagus Factory only came to be considered one of the premier examples of architectural Modernism during the 1920s, when proponents of New Architecture (*Neues Bauen*) in the circle around Gropius began to develop their own sense of tradition. At that time, Gropius espoused a complicated theory that he had adopted from his teacher Behrens. A building's purpose, its functional form, had to be elevated to the level of an art form, enabling the building to reflect the spirit of its time. The union of art and technology, that Gropius was to call for in conjunction with the Bauhaus, had its origins here. In art and technology Gropius saw the greatest dichotomy of the age, one often equated with that of "culture and civilisation" in then contemporary discussions. He considered reconciling them to be an architect's task and believed that architecture should reflect the *Zeitgeist*. Gropius linked the concept of *Zeitgeist*, ubiquitous at the time, to *Kunstwollen* (the artist's will to form), a term borrowed from the art historian Alois Riegl, who used it to designate the subconscious principle in the creation of art.

As a Werkbund architect, Gropius also thought in terms of styles. A new monumental style had to be developed by forcibly combining technical and art forms. This approach is important because it allowed Gropius to overcome the historical justifications for architectural styles, still routinely taught, and replace them with principles like *Zeitgeist, Kunstwollen,* and "art and technology". His ahistorical perspective, which was to become the perspective of Modernism, enabled him to accept the approaches of modern artists like Kandinsky, Klee, and Itten in the early years of the Bauhaus, artists who no longer derived painting from tradition, but likewise developed their own formal concepts. Gropius had abandoned the study of architecture after five semesters because of a vague feeling of apprehension he had even as a student. He considered the history taught in architectural programmes to be unnecessary ballast. Gropius did,

The Fagus Factory by Walter Gropius and Adolf Meyer, erected in Alfeld an der Leine in 1911, is considered the functionalist antithesis to Peter Behrens's monumental approach to industrial architecture.

however, believe in timeless fundamentals in all architecture, among them the laws of proportion, beauty, and spatial distribution.

Gropius developed an idealistic understanding of his own role during these "apprenticeship" years, one in which architecture had great cultural value and the architect exhibited traits of genius linked to Friedrich Nietzsche's image of man. Inferences of this can be found in his histrionic language: "Genius alone possesses the power to affix the earthly by means of the ethereal, to reveal the unfathomable", as Gropius wrote in his 1911 essay *Monumentale Kunst und Industriebau* (Monumental Art and Industrial Architecture).

Another of Gropius's important characteristics was his emphasis on economy. In 1910 he wrote an essay (which had no further consequences), *Programm zur Gründung einer allgemeinen Hausbaugesellschaft auf künstlerisch einheitlicher Grundlage* (Program to Establish a General Housing Construction Society on a Unified Basis), in which he called for the industrialisation of housing production through the use of standard types and norm parts. He was destined never to abandon this economical-industrial approach.

In the years prior to the First World War, Gropius's ideas were hardly unique. He was, however, more rigorous than other architects in creating a synthesis of current ideas in order to design a new architecture. Also characteristic of Gropius was the compulsion he felt to promote this new approach. He defined his own position for the first time in the so-called "Werkbund Dispute" of 1914. That same year Hermann Muthesius, one of the pioneers of the organisation, proposed that the adoption of standard types suitable for industrial production was more important, in the interest of better products, than the artistic freedom of the individual. The most vehement opposition to this claim came from Henry van de Velde, who emphasised the role of the creative artist, a standpoint Gropius also endorsed.

The Roots of Artistic Radicalism

Henry van de Velde in the study of his house
Hohe Pappeln in Weimar, ca. 1908

Walter Gropius shared the experience of the First World War with the rest of his generation. The initial enthusiasm for the war as a means of defending "German power and German spirit" (Kaiser Wilhelm II) gave way to critical resignation in 1917, leaving behind a nation that was falling apart by the end of the war in 1918, one that had lost its faith in the state and felt it had been deceived. The old values and traditions embodied by the Wilhelminian Reich were shattered. The Kaiser had abdicated and new political structures were only slowly forming. The middle class had no sense of intellectual orientation.

During the war, Gropius recognised that he was only suited for a position in which he was the one in charge. In his four years of military service, Gropius, who had quickly become an officer, discovered his organisational talent and capacity for leadership. When he returned to the chaotic and crisis-ridden city of Berlin as an unemployed architect in 1918, attempting to acquire new commissions, he found a solution to his own existential crisis by making two important decisions. For one, as he wrote in a letter to his mother dated mid-March 1919, he had "completely transformed his innermost self and adjusted to the new developments taking place with such great force". For another, he had become convinced during these months that he should henceforth refrain from taking sides on political issues, while at the same time becoming a radical in terms of art—a conviction that no doubt stemmed from his involvement in the *Arbeitsrat für Kunst* (Workers' Council for Art), an association of younger artists with revolutionary sympathies. Hence in 1919, with this in mind, he resumed the negoti-

In 1919 the Bauhaus moved into the School of Arts and Crafts (1904–1911) building designed by Henry van de Velde.

Gropius as a soldier in the First World War, ca. 1916

ations, interrupted in 1916, for the post vacated by Van de Velde. Grand Duke Wilhelm Ernst of Saxony-Weimar-Eisenach had forfeited his claim to the throne a few weeks previously, on 9 November 1918. A free state had been declared, and a provisional leftist government assumed office alongside the old bureaucracy, which was still in place. In addition, the *Großherzögliche Kunstgewerbeschule* (School of Arts and Crafts), of which Gropius had originally hoped to become director, had been closed since 1915. Only the *Hochschule für bildende Künste* (Academy of Fine Arts) still existed, at which a chair for architecture was to be established. Gropius's proposal that the schools be combined and operated under the name "Bauhaus", which he himself chose, was agreed to by both authorities in the confusion of the postwar period. It was the first success of Gropius's political strategy of artistic radicalism.

Das Endziel aller bildnerischen Tätigkeit ist der Bau! Ihn zu schmücken war einst die vornehmste Aufgabe der bildenden Künste, sie waren unablösliche Bestandteile der großen Baukunst. Heute stehen sie in selbstgenügsamer Eigenheit, aus der sie erst wieder erlöst werden können durch bewußtes Mit- und Ineinanderwirken aller Werkleute untereinander. Architekten, Maler und Bildhauer müssen die vielgliedrige Gestalt des Baues in seiner Gesamtheit und in seinen Teilen wieder kennen und begreifen lernen, dann werden sich von selbst ihre Werke wieder mit architektonischem Geiste füllen, den sie in der Salonkunst verloren.

Die alten Kunstschulen vermochten diese Einheit nicht zu erzeugen, wie sollten sie auch, da Kunst nicht lehrbar ist. Sie müssen wieder in der Werkstatt aufgehen. Diese nur zeichnende und malende Welt der Musterzeichner und Kunstgewerbler muß endlich wieder eine bauende werden. Wenn der junge Mensch, der Liebe zur bildnerischen Tätigkeit in sich verspürt, wieder wie einst seine Bahn damit beginnt, ein Handwerk zu erlernen, so bleibt der unproduktive »Künstler« künftig nicht mehr zu unvollkommener Kunstübung verdammt, denn seine Fertigkeit bleibt nun dem Handwerk erhalten, wo er Vortreffliches zu leisten vermag.

Architekten, Bildhauer, Maler, wir alle müssen zum Handwerk zurück! Denn es gibt keine »Kunst von Beruf«. Es gibt keinen Wesensunterschied zwischen dem Künstler und dem Handwerker. Der Künstler ist eine Steigerung des Handwerkers. Gnade des Himmels läßt in seltenen Lichtmomenten, die jenseits seines Wollens stehen, unbewußt Kunst aus dem Werk seiner Hand erblühen, die Grundlage des Werkmäßigen aber ist unerläßlich für jeden Künstler. Dort ist der Urquell des schöpferischen Gestaltens.

Bilden wir also eine neue Zunft der Handwerker ohne die klassentrennende Anmaßung, die eine hochmütige Mauer zwischen Handwerkern und Künstlern errichten wollte! Wollen, erdenken, erschaffen wir gemeinsam den neuen Bau der Zukunft, der alles in einer Gestalt sein wird: Architektur und Plastik und Malerei, der aus Millionen Händen der Handwerker einst gen Himmel steigen wird als kristallenes Sinnbild eines neuen kommenden Glaubens.

WALTER GROPIUS.

The Bauhaus Manifesto, 1919

Lyonel Feininger created a woodcut of a cathedral for the cover of *The Bauhaus Manifesto* in 1919.

Left page:
Walter Gropius, *The Bauhaus Manifesto*, 1919

The *Bauhaus Manifesto* combined a variety of ideas on anti-academic, art school reform into a single programme. Such reforms had been under discussion in Germany for over twenty years (and already realised at some institutions). Bruno Paul had already called for a "unified art school" in 1918. In revolutionary Berlin, members of the Workers' Council for Art revamped these ideas. Adolf Behne, Bruno Taut, and Otto Bartning, with whom Gropius maintained close contact, expected architecture to take a leading role.

However, there was no consensus on how to designate such a "unified art school" until Gropius coined the term Bauhaus in 1919. Gropius had always expressed his great reservations toward the three most common types of art schools: "The department of architecture at university level, in its present form, is a stillbirth, the fifth wheel on the cart. Schools for the building trades and state workshops could provide a solution. Craftsmanship and more craftsmanship ..." (15 July 1919). In his book *Bauhaus 1919–1923*, he accused the academies that trained architects and visual artists of creating an "artistic proletariat", "unprepared for life's struggles". At schools of arts and crafts, he argued, the training fostered "dilettantism", was "irrelevant" and offered "insufficient instruction in crafts and technology".

In his *Bauhaus Manifesto* Gropius formulated the call for collaboration between artists and craftsmen as an essential demand. In doing so, he again took up the idea of synthesis dating back to his early *Werkbund* period. At that time he had been trying to overcome the contradiction between art and technology, which he equated with "culture and civilisation". The fact that he now referred to the crafts, and not to technology, was related to the impoverishment of Germany after the four years of war, during which industry had collapsed entirely.

Despite the countless changes made between 1919 and 1933, the Bauhaus was still destined to remain a driving force behind—and a model of—the process of anti-academic art school reform in the Weimar Republic. In combining the two art schools in Weimar, Gropius acted as a reformer. By adopting the name "Bauhaus" and aligning the institution with the concept of a "big building project", he employed avant-gardist strategies that painters had first established in the mid-nineteenth century in France to counteract the monopoly of the powerful academies. With Expressionism, Futurism, and Dada, the practice of publishing manifestos and forming groups had become characteristic of the avant-garde, which was always redefining itself in order to maintain its distance from everyday bourgeois existence.

The Preliminary Course

A discussion of students' work in the Preliminary Course taught by Josef Albers, 1928–1929, photo by Umbo

The Preliminary Course is still seen as one of the most important innovations in Gropius's Bauhaus curriculum. It was a mandatory course of fundamental training lasting initially one semester, and later two, subsequent to which admittance to a workshop was decided upon. The artist and teacher Johannes Itten began developing the Preliminary Course at the Bauhaus in 1919. Gropius gave him a free hand in the early semesters, since he recognised Itten as a gifted teacher. His course gave the curriculum, which had previously had very little structure, its own profile. It became mandatory in the winter semester of 1920/21.

Since Itten rejected Gropius's new orientation toward industry and productivity, he left the Bauhaus in 1923 after a brief power struggle. Gropius then thoroughly revised the Preliminary Course. As of 1924, Josef Albers taught the first and László Moholy-Nagy the second semester. In 1929, Moholy-Nagy published a book on his Preliminary Course, in the Bauhaus series, entitled *von material zu architektur*. Josef Albers taught his Preliminary Course as "craft instruction" and viewed it as "creative training". He would continue teaching the course until 1933, in a form that he constantly expanded. Hannes Meyer, the director after 1928, doubted the necessity of the course. He there-

Upper left:
Johannes Itten's Preliminary Course: Rudolf
Lutz, Cubic Sculpture

Lower left:
László Moholy-Nagy's Preliminary Course:
Corona Krause, A Study in Balance, Weimar
1924

Middle:
Josef Albers's Preliminary Course: Ursula
Schneider, *A Study in Material and a Focal
Centre*, ca. 1928

Right:
Josef Albers's Preliminary Course: Walter
Tralau, *A Work Made of Paper,* Folded and
Cut, 1926

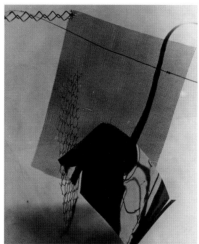

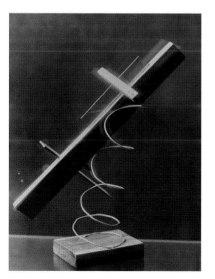

fore began, in 1930, to substitute courses in Gestalt psychology, sociology, and social economics for the Preliminary Course. Communist students called for it to be abolished entirely in 1930.

Director Mies van der Rohe decided in 1930 that the Preliminary Course was no longer mandatory. He introduced examinations at the end of every semester to decide whether students should be allowed to continue. As a result, the Preliminary Course was no longer as important as a means of selecting the most talented students, homogenising the student body, and training creativity. At the same time, he added free-hand drawing to the Preliminary Course for architects, in order to improve their ability to render designs, and assigned Albers to teach them. In 1938, when Mies van der Rohe was teaching at Chicago's Amour Institute of Technology (later called Illinois Institute of Technology), he even replaced the Preliminary Course entirely with what he called "visual training", a course intended to train students to see things in a precise, context-dependent manner. From a modern point of view, a shortcoming of the Preliminary Course was the fact that it did not include history, nature, or the environment.

Apprenticeship and Diploma

Students of the weaving class displaying the diplomas Gunta Stölzl issued as a practical joke, 1930.

Vera Meyer-Waldeck completed her carpentry exam at the Bauhaus in 1929.
Photo by Gertrud Arndt, 1930

Training to become a master craftsman was an essential part of the reform concept at the Bauhaus. Each student signed an apprenticeship contract with the *Handwerkskammer* (tradesmen's council). After an apprenticeship of three years in a workshop at the Bauhaus and successfully passing a journeyman's exam, the students became young masters. Gropius modelled this method of training on the system used by artisans and craftsmen. Around 1919 it was associated with positive aspects of the medieval building lodges of the Gothic period. Even at Weimar's *Kunstgewerbeschule* (School of Arts and Crafts) under Van der Velde, students were able to become journeymen and masters. The master model remained valid almost until the very end of the Bauhaus, although it eventually became less important. Nevertheless, in January 1932 it was still possible for Vera Meyer-Waldeck to complete her apprenticeship examination as a carpenter. In 1926, through Gropius's initiative, a clear turning point was reached: it became possible to earn a diploma. This reduced the importance of craftsman's examinations. However, the distinction between these two forms of certification was not a clear one, since they could also be earned parallel to each other. In 1930, female students in the weavers' workshop completed their journeyman's examination; shortly thereafter they celebrated receiving a Bauhaus diploma. No grades were noted on the diplomas, as was common at technical universities, instead they listed everything that the student had achieved. It neither qualified students for doctoral programmes nor for civil service as a *Regierungsbaumeister* (master builder). Almost every one of the 131 diplomas awarded was signed by Mies van der Rohe.

The Workshops

For Walter Gropius the workshops represented, in many respects, the core of training at the Bauhaus. According to the original concept, students were supposed to successfully complete workshop training before being allowed to study architecture. Since a department of architecture only existed during the last year of Gropius's tenure as director, from 1927 to 1928, the practicality of this idea could never be tested. Thus, in terms of the education it offered, Gropius's Bauhaus was a reformed school of arts and crafts.

At the Weimar Bauhaus there were workshops for glass, pottery, weaving, metal, carpentry, and wall painting, as well as wood and stone sculpture. In addition, there were stage, printmaking, and bookbinding workshops. In Dessau, these workshops were either combined, renamed, or abolished after 1925. Seven workshops remained: for metal, woodworking, textiles, wall painting, printing/advertising, sculpture, and the stage. When the Bauhaus began offering training in architecture in 1927, three other courses of study were also established: advertising, stage, and art. It also became easier to gain admittance to the architectural course; now only one year in a workshop was required and architecture became just one of a number of courses of study. Many students left the Bauhaus as journeymen, or with a diploma, without ever having come into contact with architecture. This tendency became even more pronounced under Hannes Meyer.

Hannes Meyer began reforming the workshops as soon as he became director in 1928. In 1929 he combined metalworking, carpentry, and wall painting in a workshop for interior design. The textiles workshop remained independent. He did away with the stage workshop when Oskar Schlemmer, its head, left the Bauhaus in 1929. He also established a new workshop for photography, intending to combine it with printing/advertising and sculpture, in order to form a single workshop for advertising. Under Meyer, the Bauhaus served both to train designers as well as architects.

These developments were halted by Mies van der Rohe when he abolished the apprenticeship system in 1930, thereby intensifying the link between workshop training and architecture. In addition, it became possible to study architecture without having taken the Preliminary Course or having participated in a workshop. Mies van der Rohe's curriculum from 1930 listed the following workshops and areas of training: "1. building and interior design, 2. advertising, 3. photography, 4. weaving, 5. visual art". With this orientation the Bauhaus under Mies van der Rohe was on its way to becoming a school solely for architecture.

The fundamental problem with the workshops was that their goals were contradictory: on the one hand, participation in the workshops represented a pedagogical principle, on the other hand, the workshops were expected to generate income and prototypes for eventual production.

The weaving workshop in Weimar, 1923

The Bauhaus pottery workshop located in
the stables at Dornburg Castle in 1923

The sculpture workshop in Weimar, 1923

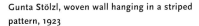
Gunta Stölzl, woven wall hanging in a striped pattern, 1923

Form Training—Craft Training

The masters of the Bauhaus in Weimar, here in Klee's studio:

(from the left) Lyonel Feininger, Wassily Kandinsky, Oskar Schlemmer, Georg Muche, and Paul Klee, who were responsible for developing courses to provide form training (*Formlehre*).

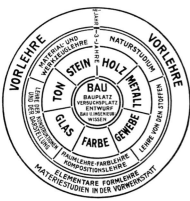

A schematic depiction of the Bauhaus curriculum, Walter Gropius, 1922

The *Bauhaus Manifesto* had announced a tripartite training system: training in drawing, crafts, and academic theory. In 1920, Gropius drew on the experience made in the first semesters when he decided—mainly on his own—that the structure of training should include both technique and form. It is fascinating to see how the masters reacted to this demand, which was repeatedly discussed at the masters' council meetings, the minutes of which are now available in print. Georg Muche, Lyonel Feininger, and Gerhard Marcks rejected the idea of *Formlehre* (form training) for diverse reasons.

However, all of the other teachers modified their courses: Lothar Schreyer taught form in calligraphy and typography (*Schriftformlehre*), Paul Klee developed a way of teaching pictorial form (*bildnerische Formlehre*), and Gropius spatial relationships (*Raumlehre*). Wassily Kandinsky taught "Fundamental Elements of Form", a "Colour Course" and figurative drawing. László Moholy-Nagy and Oskar Schlemmer also offered condensed introductions to the theories on which their artistic concepts were based. Johannes Itten, who was the first to establish a course of this kind and would have gladly continued on alone, only reluctantly made way for other teachers.

This form training (*Formlehre*), along with the training in craftsmanship provided in the workshops, was the educational backbone of the Bauhaus under Gropius. It took the place of courses in historical styles, or on drawing classical statuary and decorative ornaments from plaster models, common in other art schools. Josef Albers expressed support for Gropius's programme in a special issue of *Junge Menschen* in 1924, arguing that "a knowledge of history impedes production". Nevertheless, history was, of

1921 Johannes Itten published a colour circle depicting twelve tones in seven different shades.

Below:
Andor Weininger's *Composition with proportional figure* **reflects the combined influence of Oskar Schlemmer and Theo van Doesburg, 1923**

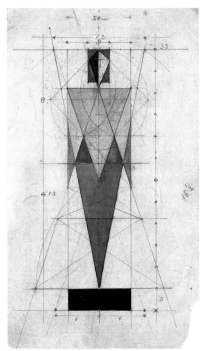

course, not entirely prohibited at the Bauhaus. There was a library, a number of journals were subscribed to, and there was some instruction in art history. But all design work at the Gropius Bauhaus was based on training that focussed on basic forms and primary colours. Hannes Meyer distanced himself decisively from all manner of training in form in 1928, and Mies van der Rohe also considered it superfluous.

Masters and Young Masters

Johannes Itten, *Portrait of a Child,* 1921/22

Altogether nine artists were appointed to teach at the Bauhaus in Weimar. One was the sculptor Gerhard Marcks (1919); the others were painters: Lyonel Feininger (1919), Johannes Itten (1919), Georg Muche (1920), Oskar Schlemmer (1921), Paul Klee (1921), Lothar Schreyer (1921), Wassily Kandinsky (1922), and László Moholy-Nagy (1923). Their spheres of influence took very different forms.

By 1921/22 esoteric models of living and working had become closely linked. Johannes Itten and Georg Muche were followers of the *Mazdaznan* movement and worked toward fulfilling the ideal of the "new man", drawing many students in their wake. The teachings of the sect prescribed breathing exercises and a vegetarian diet, and it promised a higher consciousness to those who lived properly. Itten integrated these doctrines into his art and his own teaching. In 1921 he completed an ambitious painting in which his son Matthias, born in 1920, is depicted in a context of symbolic colours and astrological signs as a stylised allegory of future expectations.

From 1919 to 1924, the music teacher Gertrud Grunow gave students individual lessons based on her theory of harmonisation, in order to determine their talent for crafts. She saw a systematic connection between tones, colours, materials and the body. Her influence reached its peak in 1923 when she wrote an essay for the publication *Bauhaus 1919–1923.* Almost at the same time, the Masters' Council concluded that the theory of harmonisation had no discernible effect.

Itten, Muche, and Grunow continued to develop the ideals of the German "reformed living" (*Lebensreform*) movement, which took an antagonistic view of technology and urbanism. The students also brought the legacy of this movement to the Bauhaus in practices long romantic walks, trips to Italy, bathing nude, sleeping outdoors, long hair, a desire to create a union of art and life, the shared experience of all-night summer solstice celebrations and uninhibited contact between the sexes, which were all part of this.

Walter Gropius was not an adherent of the movement. In 1921 he again began to favour modern technology and to see art as a means of reconciling man with it. Even during the two years in which he had supported crafts, he viewed them merely as a means to an end. Marcks, and to an extent Itten and Muche, rejected this purely functional orientation towards the crafts and judged them to have a higher value for human development.

László Moholy-Nagy's artistic approach combined the natural and biological with technologically oriented thought. Moholy-Nagy believed man could become liberated by his artistic triumph over the technical world. He took it upon himself to study the role played by the senses of sight, touch and spatial orientation and therefore studied transparency, structure and material. Moholy-Nagy was the most versatile of the Bauhaus masters. As an artist he was not limited to any one medium. He painted and took photographs, using some of them for montages and layouts. For him the production of art was a mental process, not a question of craftsmanship. This was an approach that Feininger, Klee, Kandinsky, and Schlemmer considered divisive.

Left page:
Under Moholy-Nagy's management the metal shop developed prototypes for industrial design production.
On the left at the window Marianne Brandt, next to her Hans Przyrembel

From an historical perspective, we now tend to focus on the common elements that united these artists as members of the same generation of the avant-garde. They were convinced that they had found truths that transcended historical and cultural barriers, ones that would enable them to teach students how to create. Most of them developed pedagogical theories for the courses that students were required to attend for several semesters, which they were expected to learn and apply in their work. Klee, Kandinsky, and Schlemmer each embedded their theories in a cohesive context. Although analysis and synthesis were instrumental processes to which most of them adhered, there were also differences: Klee based his on movement, Kandinsky on sensation, Schlemmer on metaphysical man. Over the years they modified their theories somewhat, in keeping with the changing orientation of the Bauhaus.

During the 1920s, Schlemmer, Feininger, Klee, and Kandinsky advanced to become leading representatives of modern culture in the Weimar Republic. As a result of their successful teaching, these masters had in fact made themselves superfluous at the Bauhaus. The following generation of young masters—Josef Albers, Herbert Bayer, Marcel Breuer, Joost Schmidt, Hinnerk Scheper, and Gunta Stölzl—separated the theories of the masters from their artistic content and integrated these elements into their own courses. The young masters were able to apply the new conceptual approach of artists like Itten, Klee, and Kandinsky to the creative process. As of 1925, they were responsible for both the theoretical and practical direction of the workshops, often directly developing course content with an eye to its practical and professional application. This was, for example, true of new professions in the field of "graphic design" or the textile industry. They did not believe in utopian concepts and it was often their impulses that gave rise to the wave of modernisation that swept the Bauhaus in Dessau after 1925. Bayer succeeded in having DIN norms and "New Typography" introduced and Scheper developed a colour guidance system for the Bauhaus building. Breuer's furniture and interior design applied industrial aesthetics to residential spaces.

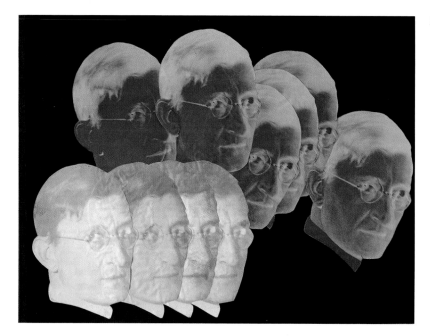

Josef Albers, *Self-Portrait Collage*, 1928

With the exception of Wassily Kandinsky, all of the "old masters" (Itten, Klee, Marcks, Moholy-Nagy, Muche, Schlemmer, and Schreyer) had left the Bauhaus by 1931.

After Gropius's departure from the Bauhaus in 1928, there were only two major educational figures—with the exception of the subsequent directors Hannes Meyer and Mies van der Rohe—who made a long-term contribution to the new profile of the school: the city planner Ludwig Hilberseimer and the photographer Walter Peterhans, both recruited in 1929. In contrast to the visual artists, who could almost all be called "generalists", they were specialists whose influence was limited to their fields of expertise.

Left:
Johannes Itten with a wooden compass in front of his colour circle
Photo by Paula Stockmar, 1920

Right:
László Moholy-Nagy wanted his work to be that of an artist-engineer and thus represented an absolute contrast to Itten's monk-like attitude.
Photo by Lucia Moholy, 1925

Women, Men, Couples

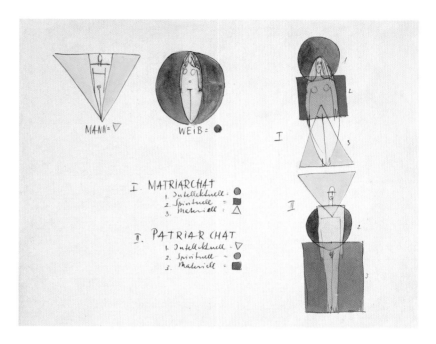

Ise Gropius, Self-Portrait, 1927

There was, on the whole, little change in the role of women at the Bauhaus. Traditional gender models persisted, in which women were "natural beings" and men "cultural beings". Children and housework were considered female domains; in terms of art, women were associated with weaving or, at most, interior design. At the Bauhaus in Weimar, the selection policy of the Masters' Council implicitly favoured male applicants. Women were assigned to the weaving workshop, which operated for a time like a "women's department". Women only made their way into other workshops through patronage or against stiff resistance.

Most of the Bauhaus masters under Gropius transmitted this bipolar concept of gender in their teachings. In a manuscript from 1920, Gropius associated the triangle with red, with the spirit and masculinity, the square with blue, with matter and femininity. In the circle, which he associated with yellow, he saw spirit and matter united. Itten, Kandinsky, Schlemmer, and van Doesburg expressed similar ideas. In 1928, Klee automatically defined genius as masculine when he compared it with "procreation" in *bauhaus,* the school's magazine. He was reflecting an intellectual tradition that went back to Nietzsche, in which creation and masculinity were nearly identical. The number of female applicants, which accounted for nearly 50 percent in the early Weimar period, gradually sank to a level of roughly 30 percent. Hannes Meyer wanted to increase the overall number of students in 1929. In his Bauhaus brochure *junge menschen kommt ans bauhaus*, he directly addressed women: "Are you looking for truly equal opportunity as a student?" Nevertheless, the number of women to graduate from the architecture and interior design programmes remained low; there were only four female graduates.

Several interesting women put in only brief appearances. One was the photographer Florence Henri, who spent one semester training at the Bauhaus, another was Erna Niemeyer, who later became famous as an author and photographer under the name Ré Soupault. Relegated to the weaving workshop, she was unable to develop her potential. Lucia Moholy and Ise Gropius successfully, but virtually invisibly, furthered the interests of the Bauhaus. Each of them was one half of what Klaus Theweleit has termed a "productive couple". Lucia Moholy, László Moholy-Nagy's wife, had trained as an editor and completed her training as a photographer in Weimar. In hundreds of photographs she documented almost every object designed at the Weimar Bauhaus, and later the "Bauhaus buildings" in Dessau. She developed a photographic style that expressed the programmatic approach of Bauhaus aesthetics. As a result of their thousand-fold circulation, these photographs have come to determine our image of the Bauhaus. Lucia also did the photo lab work for Moholy-Nagy, in addition to editing a number of Bauhaus books. Seen merely as an assistant in the context of Bauhaus history, Lucia Moholy's achievements have been insufficiently recognised.

Ise Gropius kept a similarly low profile, although in a different role. In 1923, the 40-year-old Gropius married Ise Buchard, then 26. As a young woman she soon identified herself with the Bauhaus. She wrote a still unpublished journal at her typewriter in which she combined her personal story with that of the Bauhaus. She compiled speeches and articles for Gropius based on his manuscripts and served as a Bauhaus hostess and ambassadress. She coordinated the requests made by the masters' wives while the interiors of the masters' houses were being finished. During Gropius' lifetime she was to write thousands of letters for him and continued to act on his behalf after his death in 1969. In the end, her handwriting and his were nearly indistinguishable. Each husband expressed this productive symbiosis in his own way: Moholy-Nagy and his wife created a double self-portrait in 1923, depicting their heads in a photogram. Walter and Ise Gropius worked, from 1926 on, at a double desk. The price both women paid for working in the shadow of their influential husbands was that their names disappeared behind those of their partners, and their own achievements were never really recognised

As of 1925, Mies van der Rohe and Lily Reich often formed this sort of "productive couple". In 1931 they demonstrated their bond by jointly signing furniture they had designed. Pieces featured in a brochure published by the Bamberg Metal workshops were differentiated as either "LR" or "MR". At the Berlin Building Exhibition in 1931, a wall connected Mies's bachelor's home and a house designed by Reich. She was, however, unable to share Mies's fame, since their cooperation ended with his emigration in 1938.

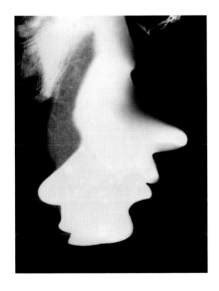

László Moholy-Nagy and Lucia Moholy, double self-portrait as a photogram, 1926

From Expressionism to Constructivism

Right:

Constructivist and Dadaist Conference in Weimar, September 1922
From the back: Lucia Moholy, Alfréd Kemény, László Moholy-Nagy, El Lissitzky, Lotte Burchartz, Cornelis van Eesteren, Bernhard Sturtzkopf, Max Burchartz (with child), Harry Scheibe, Theo van Doesburg, Hans Vogel, Karl Peter Röhl, Alexa Röhl, Nelly van Doesburg, Tristan Tzara, Nini Smith, Hans Arp, Werner Graeff, Hans Richter (reclining)

In describing the Bauhaus later, Walter Gropius tended to overlook its Expressionist phase from 1919 to 1921, negating the influence of the De Stijl movement almost entirely. With his 1923 call for "Art and Technology—A New Unity" Gropius initiated a new orientation at the Bauhaus, one that remained valid until 1928. The actual turning point for the Bauhaus came in 1922, with the first precursors of this development making themselves felt as early as 1921. An initial indication was the change in its logo in the autumn of 1921, from Karl Peter Röhl's Expressionist Bauhaus temple, featuring a "stick figure" at the centre, to Oskar Schlemmer's Constructivist head.

The medieval cult, symbolised by the Feininger woodcut on the cover of the *Bauhaus Manifesto*, was now dated. Expressionism, more political from 1918 on—as in "the cathedral of socialism"—began to seem less convincing than the seemingly more rational concepts of the Dutch De Stijl movement, founded in part by the painter and theoretician Theo van Doesburg, who had been working to popularise the movement in Germany since 1920/21. His contacts to Gropius, Fred Forbat and Adolf Meyer, both of whom were employed in Gropius's architectural office, dated back to December 1920.

Doesburg had been living in Weimar since April 1921 and had virtually besieged the Bauhaus by giving lectures, staging discussions, offering De Stijl courses, visiting the workshops, exhibiting his own work, and by publishing critiques of the Bauhaus in the magazine *De Stijl* (then published in Weimar). He also arranged visits by other De Stijl

Right:
Theo van Doesburg, *Colour Construction in the Fourth Dimension of Space-Time,* **1924**
Ink and gouache

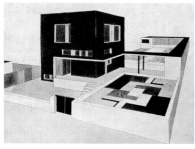

Farkas Molnár, design for a house called "The Red Cube", 1923

artists such as C. Van Eesteren and J.J.P. Oud, and held a conference for Dadaists and Constructivists in September 1922. All of this left a lasting impression on the masters and students of the Bauhaus.

Doesburg rejected the crafts, which had been emphasised at the Bauhaus up until that point, and called for machines to be used in creating modern living environments. The machine has the "capability of a pure and defined form", as J. J. P. Oud explained in the first issue of *De Stijl* in 1917. "Mechanical aesthetics" needed to be developed. Artists should not be allowed to depict their internal conflicts or their feelings, but instead should recognize their responsibility to create a world of uniform design. The material that Doesburg permitted artists to use was restricted. Only the primary colours—red, blue and yellow—along with the non-colours—black, white and grey— should be used to delineate flat, rectangular planes. Creative design entailed striking a balance between contrasting means of expression: black and white, yellow and blue, horizontal and vertical, empty and solid.

Inspired by the Bauhaus programme, Doesburg draughted what he called a "thorough bass" for architecture, sculpture, and painting in 1922. He assigned colour the function of defining space, an idea that inspired the wall painting workshop in particular. Farkas Molnár's 1922/23 Red Cube house design is inconceivable without the foregoing De Stijl influence.

Doesburg's theory was a condensate drawn from various sources. An equilibrium between polarities would allow truth and beauty to become manifest in the universe,

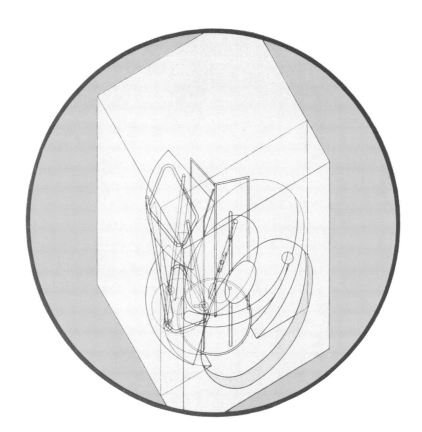

Right:

László Moholy-Nagy worked on "Light Prop for an Electric Stage" from 1922 to 1930.
Here: drawing of motion for the "Light Machine", 1930

Below:

Naum Slutzky, cubic door and handle, 1921

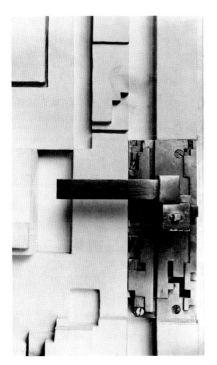

raising the art of *De Stijl* to the realm of Platonic thought. This was accompanied by a faith in the machine.

In December 1921, a group of Hungarian students, among them Marcel Breuer, distanced themselves from Expressionism with the *Kuri Manifesto*. "Kuri" stood for "constructive, utilitarian, rational, international". These new teachings also had an electrifying effect on the Bauhaus masters. Kandinsky's formerly Expressionist iconography became geometrical. Paul Klee's compositions became more rational; his application of paint and his brush technique took on a more impersonal and technical appearance. Schlemmer developed a theory of art in which he combined basic human activities such as standing, floating or walking with elemental thought, a mixture of De Stijl principles and Constructivism. When the Hungarian painter László Moholy-Nagy came to the Bauhaus in 1923 as a successor to Itten, he had already left behind his Expressionist past and his own Constructivist pictorial vocabulary. Until 1928, the Bauhaus "digested" the most diverse influences, some of which came from its own teachers and some from external sources in architecture and design, and developed its own theoretical blueprints. These were, however, then replaced by new theories when Hannes Meyer took office in 1928.

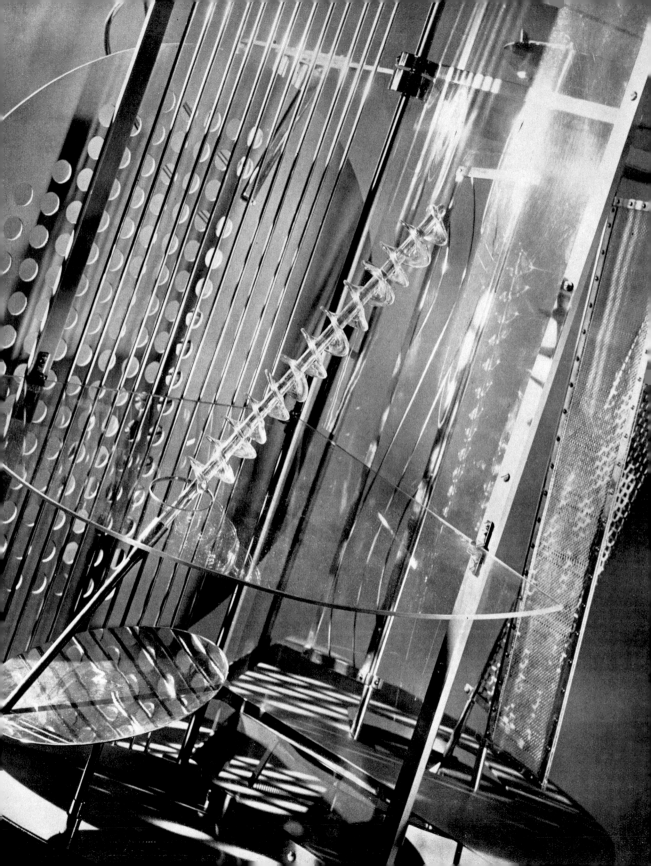

Theories of Design

Left page:
László Moholy-Nagy photographed a section of his "Light Machine", which was completed in 1930.

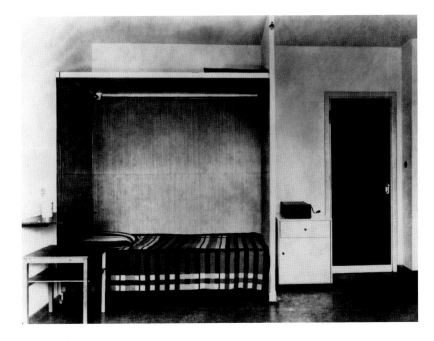

Studio rooms for students in the *Prellerhaus*
Furniture by Marcel Breuer, bedspread by Gunta Stölzl

Cabinet for a child's room, unknown designer, (M.Breuer/K. Both?, ca. 1925) in *De Stijl* style.

For as long as Gropius was director of the Bauhaus, elemental shapes and primary colours continued to be a sort of ABC for designs created in the workshops. Primary colours and elemental shapes have a long history. They can be found in nineteenth century pedagogical theories formulated by the Swiss educational theorist J. H. Pestalozzi and in the work of French pointillists; they ultimately refer back to Plato's teachings in which geometry is a reality that exists independent of man. At the Bauhaus, these elements first appeared in 1919/20 in Johannes Itten's courses. He had in part derived them from Kandinsky's book *Über das Geistige in der Kunst* (1911) and in part from the theories of Gillard and Grasset in Geneva and his teacher Adolf Hölzel in Stuttgart.

At the Bauhaus, and even earlier, different characteristics were associated with each of these primary shapes. They formed the point of departure in Klee's and Kandinsky's courses. Itten and, in part, Moholy-Nagy taught students to develop vessels by combining and interlocking primary shapes. Itten also trained the students to make use of contrasting shapes, materials and proportions. However, this theory of contrast, which exhibited purely formal parallels to Doesburg's teachings, was based on other fundamental concepts.

The theories of colour on which Itten, Klee and Kandinsky based their work were oriented on the colour systems developed by J.W. Goethe, Ph.O. Runge, and A. Hölzel. Itten and Kandinsky related their systems of colour to shapes, while Klee, on the other hand, did not. Klee's course proved particularly useful to the weavers, since he dealt with the creation of patterns by folding, mirroring, and rotating.

Here again the young masters took a pragmatic tack that was characteristic of the development of the Bauhaus. Herbert Bayer, Joost Schmidt and Hinnerk Scheper employed a scientific theory of colour based on the work of Nobel Prize winner Wilhelm Ostwald, against which Klee and Itten had protested in 1920.

In 1922, Gropius began formulating guidelines for the products of the workshops: each design was only supposed to consist of a few simple parts, so that it could easily be adapted to industrial production. As a combination of simple elements, they were also meant to lend themselves to variation. In addition, they were to be designed as standard "types". One standard chair, for example, should be sufficient for all seating requirements. In this theory, which he often publicised, Gropius again advanced his idea of synthesis as a means of bridging contradictions, in this case the economic and aesthetic conditions of a design. In 1929 the term "functionalism" began its triumphant march through the Bauhaus and was there to stay. The term was never explicitly defined there, but it did provide a framework within which the difficult balance between purpose, material and form could be expressed verbally and then projected onto real objects.

The few objects that ever actually corresponded to these somewhat contradictory demands (type, primary form, functionality) are now expensive design icons, such as the table lamp by Karl Jacob Jucker and Wilhelm Wagenfeld, the ceramic teapot by Theodor Bogler, the slatted chair by Marcel Breuer and the silver teapot by Marianne Brandt. The 1924 Jucker-Wagenfeld table lamp was available with either a metal or a glass base. The individual parts of Bogler's ceramic teapot could be re-assembled in order to form four different vessels. Breuer's slatted chair was also available in a child-sized version. Photographs of these objects were published in advertising materials where they were described as "standard types" developed on the basis of a functional analysis, so that they could be mechanically reproduced.

The aesthetics developed before Gropius's departure in 1928 are still seen as characteristic of the "Bauhaus style" today. In most cases the will to form outweighed the consideration given to proper workmanship. The objects ostentatiously demonstrate their purported functionality, which is often an aesthetic exaggeration of geometry in

Wilhelm Wagenfeld, Karl Jacob Jucker, table lamp
Metal version, 1923–1924

Right page:
Marcel Breuer, lattice chair, 1922

This photo with metal objects by Hans Przyrembel on a Bauhaus tablecloth was taken after his Bauhaus period around 1930

Left:
Max Krajewski, teaglass holder, 1924
Photo by Lucia Moholy

In 1928 Gyula Pap photographed two bowls from the metal workshop with reflections.

Gerhard Marcks, coffee machine "Sintrax", 1924

the De Stijl sense. The designs, which are usually additive, emphasise a machine-like character and stand in stark contrast to the flowing, organic forms of the *Jugendstil* objects designed by van de Velde or the industrial culture of the products designed by Peter Behrens. This is precisely why contemporaries considered them innovative.

Marcel Breuer's tubular steel chairs, originally created in 1925, still adhered to the doctrine of standard types: Breuer designed ten types of chairs and tables intended to suit every need. In addition to many others, Gropius's successors Hannes Meyer and Mies van der Rohe were particularly vocal in their fundamental criticism of this method of creating designs. In his 1930 "Open Letter", Hannes Meyer concluded, "The cube was trump, and its sides were yellow, red, blue, white, grey, black". All "access to forms of design suited to real life" is blocked. This rejection of Gropius as a "formalist" was quite likely the only point on which Meyer and Mies van der Rohe ever agreed.

Ideas for Housing Construction

A prototype of the *Haus am Horn* in Weimar, 1923
Design by the painter Georg Muche, constructed by Gropius's architectural office

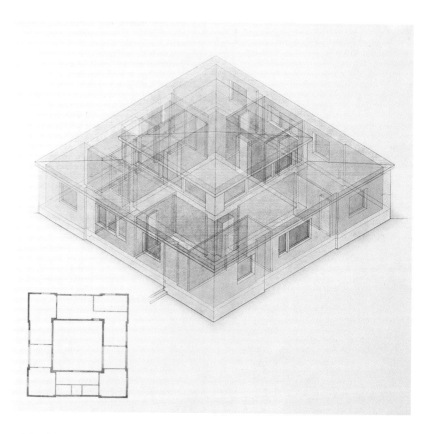

Walter Determann, design for a Bauhaus colony in a crystal pattern, Weimar 1920

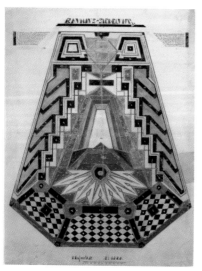

While planning the Bauhaus, Gropius also developed the idea for an artists' colony, for which the student Walter Determann submitted a design featuring Expressionistic, crystal-like forms in 1920. After the establishment of a cooperative housing society in 1922, the architect Fred Forbat was commissioned to work out initial plans, which Gropius then exhibited as a "honeycomb building" that same year. A predetermined basic unit containing the living room could be augmented by eight different prefabricated "living cells". At the Bauhaus Exhibition in 1923 this scheme was presented in a slightly altered manner as an "oversized set of building blocks". This principle, which Gropius also propagated for design, was supposed to combine both the greatest possible aesthetic variety and rationality. Doesburg's drawing of a "thorough bass" for architecture, in which four structures appear to be randomly floating around a large block, influenced these projects, since for the first time Gropius refrained from presenting a traditional rendering in elevation.

The fact that there was never a department of architecture at the Bauhaus under Gropius has always been a very sensitive matter. Many of the buildings designed in his private architectural office have been attributed to the Bauhaus, both in the literature

Haus am Horn designed as a prototype of
the ideal single-family house

Walter Gropius
"An oversized set of building blocks", 1923

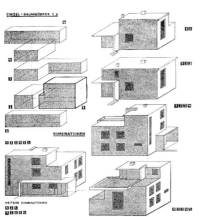

and in the public perception. This is justifiable insofar as Bauhaus students worked in Gropius's office, or Bauhaus workshops were commissioned to do the interiors in Gropius buildings. The only genuine Bauhaus building is the prototype *Haus am Horn*, based on a design by the painter Georg Muche, carried out with the help of Adolf Meyer and built for the 1923 Bauhaus Exhibition. It was planned as the ideal single-family house. Muche based the design on the "honeycomb" studies without adopting their asymmetry, choosing instead the traditional regularity of an atrium house. The building lacked the aesthetic conviction of many Bauhaus products; it only half-heartedly deferred to modernism. The decision to place a square within a square resulted in too many restrictions in terms of access. There were absolutely no corridors, the living room was the largest room and the others were only of minimal size. The architect Erich Mendelsohn commented that in this case the Bauhaus had not lived up to its potential.

The Director's Office in Weimar, 1924

Doesburg criticised the "honeycomb building" in his 1922 lecture "From New Aesthetics to Material Realisation". Cobbling together a series of building cells, he argued, could not be equated with "formative architectural design". It was this "formative architectural design" that played a central role in the conception of the director's office, completed in 1924. The room, which was reconstructed in 1999, is an homage to the square; Klaus-Jürgen Winkler and Gerhard Oschmann have shown that Gropius transformed the room, which was originally larger and higher, by using partitions and a suspended ceiling to create a cube measuring five metres by five metres. The expansive lamp, in which Gropius again addressed the theme of the cube, refers to a model by the De Stijl artist Gerrit Rietveld, while all the furnishings—from the carpet to the lighting—echo the square.

In the ensuing years, this austere sense of order, also documented in an isometric diagram, was abandoned in favour of more flexible interiors. The masters' houses are an example of this. In 1922 Gropius developed a hierarchical theory of space: first it was necessary to come to terms with tangibly material space and then with mathematically constructed space, in order to ultimately reach transcendental space. Only by coming to terms with these three dimensions was it possible to create artistic space. In formulating a justification for this spatial theory, Gropius referred to Grunow, Itten, and Le Corbusier. The director's office can be seen as a demonstration of his theory.

Herbert Bayer, axonometric projection of the director's office, 1923

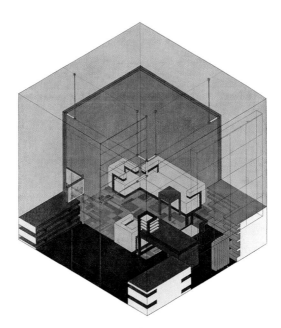

Left page:
Walter Gropius, director's office in Weimar, ca. 1924
Photo by Lucia Moholy, hand-coloured print

The Bauhaus Building in Dessau, 1925–1926

Left page:

Walter Gropius, Bauhaus building in Dessau
View through the fully glazed corner of the
workshop wing, 1927. Photo by Lucia Moholy

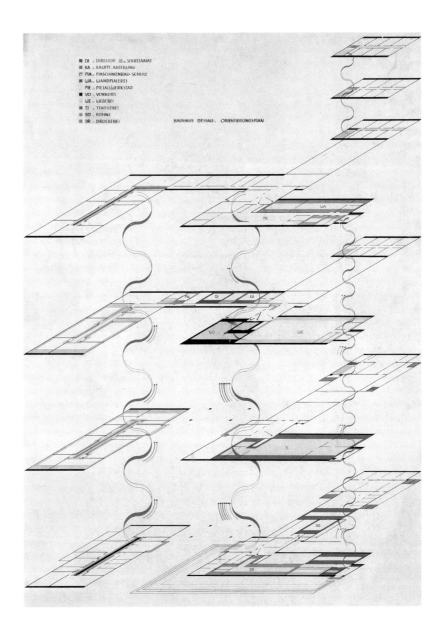

In his orientation plan, Hinnerk Scheper
assigned different colours to each part of the
Bauhaus building.
Drawing from 1926

Entrance to the assembly hall with light fixtures

Between 1925 and 1928, Gropius was able to execute three different building projects in Dessau: the school building, the masters' houses and the Törten Housing Estate. In 1930, Gropius published a description of these buildings, erected by his architectural office, under the title *bauhausbauten dessau*, a designation that became common currency. There is no doubt that Gropius, who made appearences all over Germany as the preacher of a new life style, built the "Bauhaus buildings" as a demonstration of New Architecture.

The Bauhaus building does not have a traditional façade; instead, it extends in three directions forming an L. The complex includes workshops, the studio building, the bridge where the administration and the architectural office were located, as well as a building section for the technical school, which was not connected to the Bauhaus. The individual design of each of these buildings was intended to provide an external indication of their different internal functions. At the same time the horizontal and vertical structures were carefully balanced to form an asymmetric, "dynamic" equilibrium. By creating a balance between separate structures, and between the internal and the overall space, Gropius was able to revive his old vision of reconciliation between man and technology in this individual interpretation of Doesburg's De Stijl principles.

Here Gropius treated space differently than he had in the 1924 director's office. At that time he had based his spatial theory on an imaginary individual, now he was propagating an "altered sense of space" that would reflect the mobility of the age, "These buildings seem to be imbued with a sense of buoyancy, weightlessness and rhythmic mobility". This was made possible by new building materials such as iron, concrete, and glass.

Even the ground plan is laid out in De Stijl style, something probably inspired by Mies van der Rohe. In 1923 Gropius had asked Mies to draw up a plan for his "country

Right:
View of glass façade of the Bauhaus building with lettering designed by Herbert Bayer

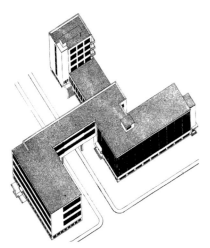

house in ferroconcrete"; its axes that extend in three directions are echoed in the Bauhaus building. The huge letters spelling out "Bauhaus", designed by Herbert Bayer, turned the architecture into an "advertising medium".

Along with the Fagus Factory, the Bauhaus building is considered Gropius's most convincing project, while the masters' houses, completed shortly thereafter, and the Törten Housing Estate have often been subject to criticism.

The Masters' Houses in Dessau, 1925–1926

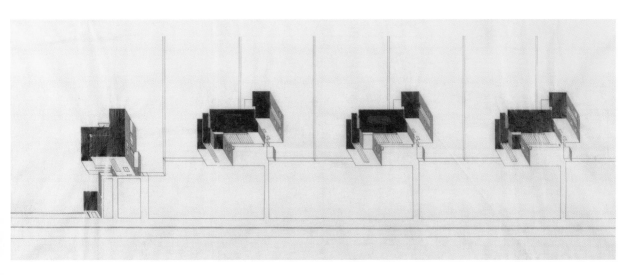

Isometric projection of the entire complex
On the left the Gropius house (destroyed during the war), next to it the two-family houses Feininger/Moholy, (the Moholy half destroyed in the war), Muche/Schlemmer, and Klee/Kandinsky

Left page:
View of the masters' houses from outside
Photo by Lucia Moholy

With the completion of the masters' houses in 1926, encompassing a single-family house for Gropius and three two-family houses for the families Klee and Kandinsky, Muche and Schlemmer, and Moholy-Nagy and Feininger, Gropius had finally had an opportunity to actually test his ideas on rationalisation in residential construction. He used one floor plan for all the semi-detached houses; only his own house is laid out differently. On the ground floor of the semi-detached houses there was a living room and a smaller dining room with a well-equipped kitchen adjoining it, including a built-in sideboard and a pantry. The greatest luxury in the semi-detached houses may have been the spacious studios on the first floor. Each of the semi-detached houses was equipped with a veranda and balconies.

In Gropius's single-family house, the most important rooms were located on the ground floor; the living room that also served as an office could be opened up to the adjoining dining room in order to create a larger space. From each of these rooms it was possible to step out onto the veranda. The floor plans have often been considered too conventional, and the large attic room at the top with a highly desirable southwest orientation was also subject to criticism.

Gropius designed the exterior as a series of interlocking cubes. Here again the principles of load distribution applied in traditional architecture were redefined in the spirit of De Stijl, namely as a balance between vertical and horizontal forces. Hannes Meyer referred to the masters' houses as "inspired neo-sculptural structures".

Mies van der Rohe eradicated the memory of the house's first resident, Gropius, by redecorating the large living and dining area on the ground floor in an entirely different manner.

Gropius's house
View from the south. Photo by Lucia Moholy

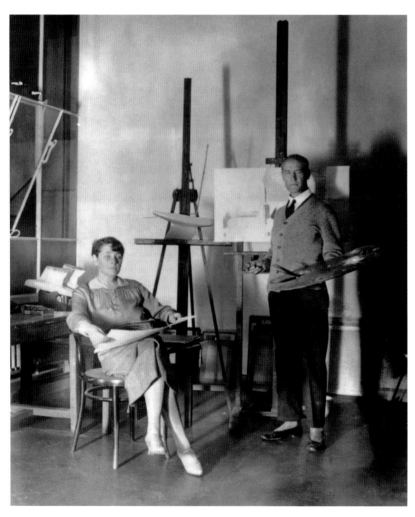

Lyonel and Julia Feininger in the studio of
their master's house in Dessau, ca. 1927

Klee and Kandinsky drinking tea outside of the masters' houses.

Klee's house

Stairway on the upper floor of the master's house with the paint restored

The Housing Estate in Dessau-Törten, 1926–1928

The houses of the Törten Housing Estate (Dessau) also serve as an aesthetic demonstration of rationalised construction.

The housing shortage was one of the greatest challenges facing the Weimar Republic. The city of Dessau's decision to ask the Bauhaus to relocate to the city was partly motivated by the desire to commission the institute with the planning and construction of new housing. The first commission came in 1926. Gropius's architectural office built the Törten Housing Estate in Dessau, consisting of 314 small, two-storey single-family houses, which were built in three phases between 1926 and 1928 on small parcels of land. Gropius wanted to use this commission to demonstrate the advantages of industrialising the construction process. To this end, all of the tasks at the construction site were organised according to the principle of assembly-line production developed in the United States. The serial aesthetics of the estate reflect the production method.

The residents, who were also owners, accepted the modern architecture more or less indifferently, while they were clearly embittered by construction flaws and cost overruns. The monotonous slab housing blocks, primarily a consequence of the implementation of cranes, afforded many of the residents in the ring streets and the double row of houses to the south little direct sun. Despite the fact that a building for a shopping cooperative was included in the plan, it never really became the centre of the estate, which lacked urban amenities. During Hannes Meyer's tenure, students criti-

The consumers' cooperative was intended as a focal point in the semi-rural estate (Walter Gropius, 1928).

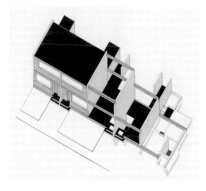

Construction plan of the first house type built at the Törten Housing Estate in 1926

cised the entrances to the houses built in the second phase as: "Black rectangles squeezed into the corner without any roof for protection", according to by Philipp Tolziner, a former Bauhaus student.

In Dessau, Gropius developed three different modes of expression for the New Architecture: pathos and asceticism in the Bauhaus building, a disciplined display of bourgeois values in the masters' houses, and manifest simplicity in the houses of the Törten Housing Estate. In the history of architecture one often finds examples that correspond with the different demands placed upon these buildings: the Bauhaus building commanded the respect due a public edifice. The masters' houses expressed a sense of a modern bourgeois desire for recognition. People of smaller means were expected to settle for simplicity and uniformity.

New Residential Architecture

Karl Hubbuch
Martha, ca. 1927

Left page:
Gymnastics room in the sports teacher's flat in Berlin
Interior by Marcel Breuer and Gustav Hassenpflug, 1929

By exhibiting the prototype *Haus am Horn* in 1923, the Bauhaus was able to realise one of its most important goals for the first time: that art must change life. A new solution for literally every detail of the house had been found in the workshops through the symbiosis of art and technology. The skirting boards and windowsills were made of black opak glass; each piece of furniture had been specially designed and a number carpets knotted. The traditional sofa had to make room for a bench without a backrest. Instead of wooden cabinetry in the living room, there was a glass display case in the corner. Particular care had been taken in the nursery, which featured mobile, colourful furniture. The kitchen was quite likely the first modern working kitchen in Germany. Using pictures as a form of decoration was discouraged, while subtle hues were allowed for the walls. The *Haus am Horn* marked the beginning of a campaign to re-educate the public. Its goal was to overcome a tendency to collect the status symbols and creature comforts, so important to the bourgeoisie, and focus on "living economically" (Anni Albers, 1925), functionally and hygienically.

A central aspect of "the new home" was the re-organisation of functional routines, the "organisation of living processes" (W. Gropius). This was intended to help reduce the amount of living space required, make housework easier and facilitate rationalisation and standardisation in the home.

Gropius conceived the masters' houses in Dessau as an example of how these goals might be realised, thus many daily routines were determined by the floor plans. All of the cupboards and shelves were built-in. In finishing the interiors of the houses, great care was taken to include the most modern technical and electrical installations, as had also been the case in the model house in 1923, for in 1930 Gropius was of the opinion that "much of what appears to be a luxury today will be the norm in future!" The interior work was done by the Bauhaus workshops.

Breuer's tubular steel furniture, with its metallic shimmer, became a symbol of "New Living". Detractors criticised the chairs as seating machines, which were at best suited for doctors' offices. Admirers appreciated the fact that the furniture was lightweight, versatile and easily disassembled.

Gropius and Moholy-Nagy opened their model residences for viewers, and there was even a film made. Photos circulated by the Bauhaus were published in newspapers and magazines. Many of these innovations were developed further for the 1927 Weißenhof Exhibition in Stuttgart.

Living room of Lázló Moholy-Nagy's master's house
Photo by Lucia Moholy, 1927/28

Right:
The nest of tables B 9 and the folding club chair B 4, here as a replica, were part of Breuer's range of "Typenmöbel" (type furniture) which he had designed in 1925.

Tubular steel furniture by Marcel Breuer in the
living room of Walter Gropius' show house no.
16 at the Werkbund estate at Weißenhof in
Stuttgart in 1927

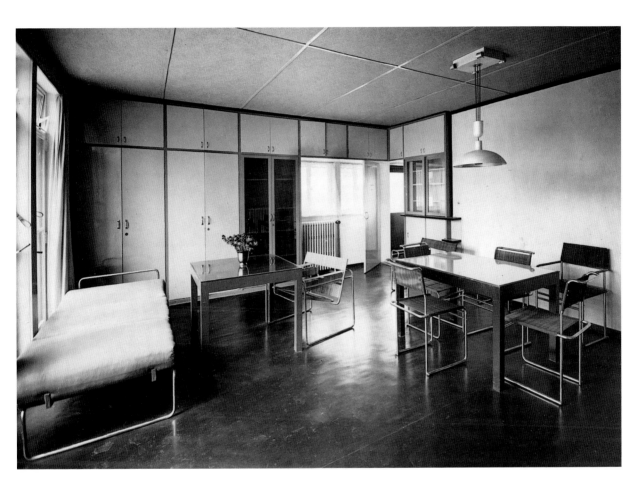

Right:
For the Thonet company Marcel Breuer
designed the successful armchair B 64 with
wickerwork and in 1928/29 the fabric-covered
armchair B 35

Reform and Avant-Garde under Gropius

The reformist, anti-academic impulse that had led to the founding of the Bauhaus in 1919 was still vital in 1928. None of the artists recruited by Gropius had ever taught at an academy before. They were recruited—incredibly—without ever discussing the workshops that were meant to be such an essential part of the anti-academic concept. The newly recruited members were initially assured that they would, for the most part, not be required to teach. Lyonel Feininger, who had a contract at the Bauhaus from 1919 to 1929, was the director of the printing workshop for several years, but never taught regularly. Georg Muche wrote in 1919 that he was only obliged to work half a day every week. "Systematic teaching is—as I hope is obvious—out of the question", as Oskar Schlemmer stated in 1920. Johannes Itten declared that the first class he taught represented a triumph over academia: "With one fell swoop I overcame the old academic tradition of life and landscape drawing and reduced artistic activity to its very roots, to a matter of playing a game." Such "games" deepened the rift between the new staff and those who had come to the Bauhaus from the former art academy in 1919).

Gropius envisioned the Bauhaus as an entity that would organise itself and evolve autonomously out of the freedom, mutual respect and cooperation of its members, thereby creating its own structures. A part of the anti-academic concept included reverting back to the use of the title "master". The masters conferred with each other in the "Masters' Council". The masters' privileges, particularly those of the "masters of form", were considerable. They earned more money and had more decision-making

December 1926, the Bauhaus masters in the connecting corridor between the second floor of the workshop building and the technical school
Left to right: W. Kandinsky and his wife Nina, Georg Muche, Paul Klee, Walter Gropius

power than the master craftsmen. In Dessau they were able to move into the spacious masters' houses in 1926, while the housing colony Bambos, planned for the "young masters" by Marcel Breuer, was never built. Muche, against whom the weavers' workshop staged a revolt in 1926, was suspended from his post for over a year at full pay. Adolf Meyer and Gertrud Grunow were even given the titles of "extraordinary master". In official Bauhaus publications their names were listed on the same level as those of other masters. Even Hannes Meyer and Hans Wittwer were appointed to the position of masters in 1927.

From the very beginning, the impetus for anti-academic reform was combined with elitist and avant-garde tendencies. In 1919 Gropius had wanted to establish a "community of kindred spirits". He was thinking of a "small, secret, exclusive brotherhood, order, lodge or conspiracy dedicated to preserving a common mystery, a core of belief". Gropius's resolution to become an artistic radical in 1919 obviously stemmed from his encountering radical, avant-garde standpoints in the Workers' Council for Art. Moholy-Nagy also brought experience with the strategies of the new Constructivist avant-garde with him in 1923. In 1922 he had co-edited the *Buch neuer Künstler* (Book of New Artists), which was a handbook on new tendencies in art. Many of the projects at the Gropius Bauhaus echoed the practices of avant-garde groups. The publication of *Mappenwerke europäischer Graphik* (Portfolio of European Graphic Art), begun in 1921, and the Bauhaus book series, begun in 1925, were intended to rally the forces of Modernism around the Bauhaus banner. Artist's groups like *Die Brücke* in Dresden and *Der Blaue Reiter* in Munich had published similar manifestos, artist's books, postcards and editions of graphic works before the war. The "Circle of Friends" established by Gropius in 1924, to which Albert Einstein, Marc Chagall, and Arnold Schönberg belonged, had predecessors in the circles of friends and members' circles within the artistic avant-garde.

The "New Typography", introduced at the Bauhaus by Moholy-Nagy, lent texts an appearance as radical as the demands they made. In 1923, Gropius organised an architectural exhibition called *Internationale Architektur*. In doing so, he was the first person in Germany to relate architecture to the artistic avant-garde's tendency toward internationalisation. With the founding of a Bauhaus magazine in 1926, the school launched into the sort of missionary activity found in other avant-garde groups.

The Bauhaus building in Dessau can be seen as an ideal location for the avant-garde elite. There was space to work in the studios and workshops, a stage for festivities, a cafeteria to provide food and even a laundry. The assembly hall at the Dessau Bauhaus, with its 164 seats, and the Preller Building, with its 28 studio rooms, give some indication of what Gropius thought of as the ideal size of the staff and student body. In one important point, however, Gropius set aside elitist tendencies: the Bauhaus was open to journeymen; a formal qualification for university study was not required. When Moholy-Nagy declared in *von material zu architektur* that "each and every person is talented", Gropius did not disagree, even if the strict selection process in the Preliminary Course did in fact tend to filter out all but the elite, proving that many of the applicants were simply not talented enough.

The duality of reform and avant-gardism was in evidence at the Bauhaus from the very beginning. As the first institution in the Weimar Republic to address the long-standing call for art school reform, the Bauhaus sought to join together with similar schools. In 1930, two years after he had placed the direction of the school in other hands, Gropius still claimed, in his introduction to *bauhausbauten dessau*, that the Bauhaus was "obligated to take the lead" in firmly establishing an "anti-academic orientation" at art schools. However, the avant-garde approach at Gropius's Bauhaus went beyond the measure of other reformed art schools and developed an ever greater consciousness of its own worth. In 1920 Gropius defined one of the Bauhaus's goals to be that of serving as a model for other schools. This model character was nourished by the sense of elitism shared by the artists gathered there. In 1922, for example, the masters refused to accept the title of professor, one that commanded considerable prestige in bourgeois circles. In 1924 they also handed in their resignations to the state of Thuringia, even though this was not legally possible.

Under Gropius, the Bauhaus oscillated between reform and avant-garde practices that would have been unusual at any school, thereby postulating programmatic standpoints that were often a step ahead of reality. Even Gropius's famous call for "Art and Technology: A New Unity" in 1923 had the character of a manifesto that transcended the reality of everyday life. The criticism lodged by many architects with regard to the Bauhaus—among them Bruno Taut and Ernst May—focussed on the "space for possibilities" to which its chief theoretician laid claim. Gropius had ensured intellectual freedom at the institution from the very beginning, and preserved it successfully through his hiring policies and wise leadership. An assessment of the situation around 1928 shows that these advantages stood in contrast to a number of disadvantages: a chronic shortage of money, the lack of a department of architecture, political attacks, and internal problems.

Curriculum of the Bauhaus Dessau, 1925
Design by Herbert Bayer

Hannes Meyer, Director, 1928–1930

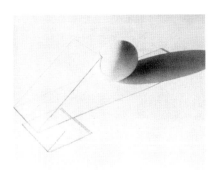

Hannes Meyer, "Co-op Construction" made of panes of glass and an egg, 1926

A new phase in the history of the Bauhaus began when Hannes Meyer (1889–1954) became director. Gropius's decision to resign from his contract in March 1928 was precipitated mainly by economic and organisational problems that marred his relationship to Dessau's mayor Fritz Hesse, the Bauhaus's most important political supporter.

Gropius had been forced to agree to a very tight budget when he signed the contract in 1925. As a result, funding was extremely limited; the income from tuition fees and workshop products was lower than expected; the salary paid to the school's legal council was too high, and the expenditures for the Bauhaus building and the masters' houses overran the estimates. Flaws in construction and rising costs at the Törten Housing Estate had caused controversy in Dessau for years. Even Gropius's frequent absence became a political issue.

For barely a year, from April 1927 to March 1928, Walter Gropius and Hannes Meyer worked together at the Bauhaus. Gropius met Meyer in December 1926 and appointed him as director of the newly established architectural programme. In August 1927 Meyer's partner of two years, the Swiss architect Hans Wittwer, came to assist him. Gropius later claimed that Meyer had been a closet communist when he took office. But in fact Meyer was most at home in the Swiss cooperative movement, for which he had designed the Freidorf colony in 1919/20. He was so impressed by the movement that he adopted the pseudonym "co-op". In 1924 he joined a radical Swiss architects' group centred around the magazine ABC, which drew his attention to the international movement called New Architecture. With two highly acclaimed architectural projects—their entries for competitions to design the Peterschule in Basel in 1926 and the League of Nations Palace in Geneva in 1927—Meyer/Wittwer had made a name for themselves within this movement.

For the new Peterschule building in the narrow streets of Basel the architects proposed a schoolyard on a surface suspended from the building by four massive steel cables. In their design for the League of Nations Building they combined a parabolic assembly hall with two twenty-four-storey, H-shaped, high-rise office buildings. The aerial image of the design is reminiscent of the dramatic staging Meyer used for his "co-op" photographs, made at the same time.

When Gropius prepared the second edition of his book *Internationale Architektur*, in the spring of 1927, he paid his respects to the director of the department of architecture by featuring a photo of Meyer/Wittwer's design for the League of Nations on the page opposite a photograph of the Bauhaus building.

In the essay *Die Neue Welt*, in which Hannes Meyer summarised some of his travelling experiences in 1926, he sketched a euphoric vision of the future. It is reflected in the spirit of his designs for a "new man", who he saw taking advantage of a range of technical innovations: airplanes, gramophones, synthetic building material,s and standardised products. He made a case for seeing houses as "machinery for living" that could help to reduce the housewife's burden and create more time for family life. The new "pervasive role of science in the world around us" enriches life, allowing it to be

Left page:
Hannes Meyer with two students on the Bauhaus terrace

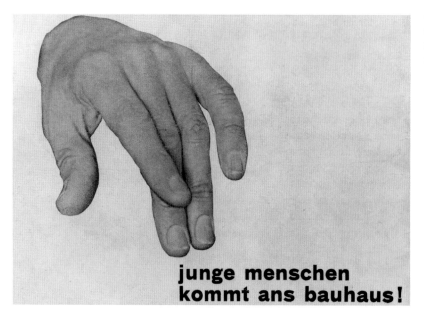

junge menschen
kommt ans bauhaus!

arranged more consciously. This was Meyer's standpoint when he was appointed director of the Bauhaus. He took office on 1 April 1928.

An initial course correction, quite obviously meant for the public's benefit as well, took place in 1929, the year of the school's tenth anniversary. In the year's first issue of *bauhaus*, Meyer published the manifesto "Bauhaus and Society", alluding portentously to Walter Gropius's *Bauhaus Manifesto* of 1919. "The final objective of all formative activity is the building!" was Gropius's opening sentence. Meyer reformulated it to state: "the final objective of all work at the Bauhaus is the coordination of all life-inducing forces to promote the harmonious formation of our society." Meyer introduced two themes in this text that were new within the context of the Bauhaus. The first can be designated by the term "the people". He called for "people's schools, people's gardens, and people's houses" as well as knowledge of the "people's traditional lifestyle, the people's soul and the community of the people". The second was related to "landscape". He emphasised that every form of design must also consider the surrounding landscape and concluded: "as designers we determine the fate of the landscape." In his call for "harmony" both of these standpoints intersected. With this, Meyer distanced himself clearly from the standpoint of the technically enthusiastic internationalists with whom he had identified himself in the years before 1929. His technologically oriented image of man was displaced by one that was now oriented toward social biology.

Despite these shifts one question always concerned Meyer: the role of art in the design process. In his texts, he categorically rejected the involvement of art: "Building structures evolve automatically", he wrote in the *Die Neue Welt* and in the *Bauhaus* magazine 1928/4: "building is a biological process. building is not an aesthetic process." If needs have been scientifically determined, then the form of the building will follow on its own. However, practice and theory diverged in Meyer's case: the Peterschule and League of Nations were "based on science", yet their appearance was clearly influenced by the aesthetics of Constructivist engineering. Meyer was still an

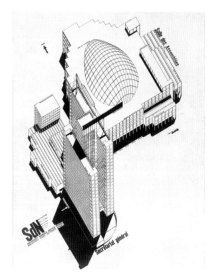

Hannes Meyer, Hans Wittwer, design for the League of Nations Building in Geneva, 1927
Axonometric projection from the southwest.

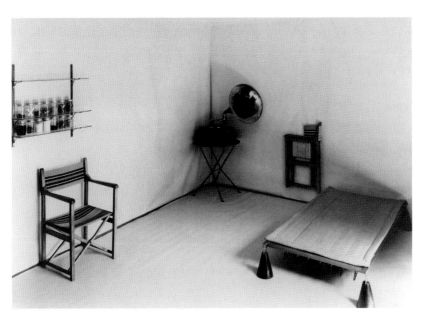

Hannes Meyer, "Co-op interior" with standardised furniture, 1924

artist, and this not only as an architect. His most important texts were published in the artistic form of the manifesto. He did not give up his pseudonym "co-op" until 1930. He often explained that there were two kinds of art. One kind that was identical to creating order and structure, hence part of the solution, while every other kind of art was basically superfluous.

Rather than attempting to address these contradictions in a fruitful dialogue, Meyer sought a clear-cut solution. He wanted to compile his findings in order to create "an exact system", as he wrote to Adolf Behne in January 1928. His assessment of the different Bauhaus artists varied: he admired some of them personally, like Paul Klee, while discrediting others as representatives of "outmoded theories of art". In 1930 Meyer went one step too far when he publicly espoused Marxism. Meyer's many re-orientations, and his constant scepticism with regard to art, fuelled conflicts that led to his being fired without notice in August 1930.

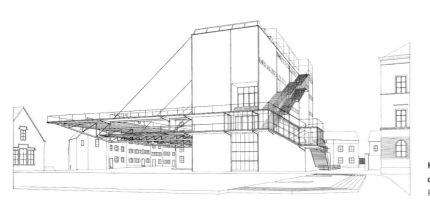

Hannes Meyer and Hans Wittwer, proposed design for the Petersschule, Basle
Perspective of the reworked version, 1927

Changes among the Masters

Walter Peterhans, around 1930
Photographed by his student Grete Stern

Left page:
Ludwig Hilberseimer standing in front of a model for his "Welfare City" consisting of six fifteen-storey towers, 1927

In 1928—at almost the same time as Gropius—Marcel Breuer, Herbert Bayer and László Moholy-Nagy resigned. Feininger began teaching in Halle in May 1929, but continued to live in his master's house. In July 1929 Schlemmer left the Bauhaus, followed in May 1930 by Klee, who informed Hannes Meyer that he was leavingfor the academy in Düsseldorf. This exodus of old and young masters allowed Meyer to recruit new staff, including the most important additions, Ludwig Hilberseimer and Walter Peterhans.

In 1922, Hilberseimer called for the "reduction of architectural forms to the sparest, most essential, most general" in *Das Kunstblatt*. Every aspect of design and planning was based on systematic calculations. As a city planner he developed solutions in which high-rise construction could be used to create greater urban density. He systematically examined the relationship between residential density and building types, for example the high-rises vs. the single-family house. He drew a connection between optimally planning individual building sites and city planning on the whole. Gropius had also considered such problems, but never dealt with them in the classroom. Hilberseimer's pragmatism and rational, socio-political approach to solving housing problems corresponded ideally with Meyer's programme. Hilberseimer's objective radicalism, in which he consciously avoided aesthetic considerations, made him a typical representative of scientifically oriented functionalism. Here the various manifestations of New Architecture can be classified in different categories. Meyer and Hilberseimer were seen as "rationalists" who were interested in social issues and rejected art. Gropius, the "formalist", made a case for industrialisation on the basis of standard types and rationalisation.

In 1929 Meyer appointed the photographer Walter Peterhans, who had completed his training at Leipzig's prestigious *Staatliche Akademie für Buchgewerbe und Graphik* (State Academy for Book Production and Graphic Art) in in 1926, after having previously studied mathematics and philosophy. Peterhans also espoused scientific approaches. According to his theory, beauty existed independently of human beings and could be reproduced by methodically developing the technical aspects of the photographic process.

Meyer, who had begun discussing the reforms he planned before taking office, organised the workshop courses between the poles of art and science. The proponents of the old theory of form training (*Formlehre*), Klee and Kandinsky, were depicted on the art side of a chart drawn up in 1929. Meyer avoided the word *Formlehre* about which he was given to making polemic statements, since for him design could never be based on formally predetermined premises. During his entire tenure in office, Meyer worked on more firmly establishing the "scientific" pole. Meyer's conceptual strength is reflected in this new orientation.

Scientific Design

Lis Beyer in the "Tütenkostüm" (bag costume) for the Weiße Fest (White Festival) in March 1926.

The wide spectrum of ideas, once found at Gropius's Bauhaus, was replaced under Meyer by three different orientations, all of them purportedly scientific. Of these, communism was historically the most consequential, claiming to be a scientific view of the world. "The student representatives are always coming with communist arguments", wrote Oskar Schlemmer on 28 January 1928 to his wife Tut. In 1930, Meyer described himself as a "scientific Marxist" to Dessau's mayor Hesse; the latter then sought his immediate dismissal.

The Swiss architect's group ABC also characterised their approach as scientific. They rejected art and supplanted it with the supposedly impersonal concept of *Gestaltung* (design). For this group Russian Constructivism represented a point of departure, it had been introduced in Germany by El Lissitzky, who visited the Bauhaus in 1923 and 1930. Their often repeated argument stated that: art is composition, but since building was not a question of composition, but rather only means to an end, building could never be an art form. Meyer propagated this thesis and the students espoused it. However, while Meyer argued the case for this radical position in his publications during his tenure at the Bauhaus, he still supported the concept of "functionalism as an art form", advanced by the Czech architectural critic Karel Teige and the Hungarian

Back of brochure of Joost Schmidt for tourist information office of the city of Dessau, 1931

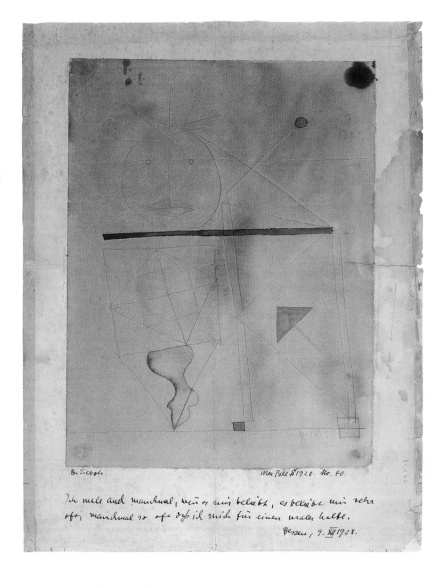

Max Bill, *Der Eilbote* (The Express Courier), 1928
Created as a free project at the Bauhaus under the influence of Paul Klee ("I sometimes paint when I feel like it, and I feel like it so often that I consider myself a painter." Dessau, 9 XII 1928)

writer Ernst Kallai. Both of them were able to present their standpoints extensively at the Bauhaus: Teige as a guest instructor in 1930, Kallai as editor of *bauhaus* magazine.

The third orientation, which claimed to be legitimated by science, was inspired by the Vienna Circle, a group of philosophers that included Rudolf Carnap, Herbert Feigl, and Walter Dubslav, who all gave lectures at the Bauhaus. These philosophers, some of whom were also mathematicians and physicists, developed a "universal science" that only accepted the given as the source of all knowledge. The economist Otto Neurath also espoused this philosophy. He introduced the students to "pictorial statistics", something he was just then developing, which used pictograms to depict social relationships.

Important aesthetic impulses came from the photographer Umbo, who rose to sudden fame in 1927 for his innovative, close-up photographic portraits. In 1928 he began taking photographs at the Bauhaus incessantly. These photographs influenced

Paul Klee, *gewagt wägend* (Daringly balanced), 1930, 144 (Y 4)
Aquarelle and pen on paper on cardboard, 13 x 24.5/23.5 cm

Karla Grosch doing floor exercises with students on the roof of the Prellerhaus, Dessau ca. 1930.

Hannes Meyer's use of the medium in the 1929 brochure *junge menschen kommt ans bauhaus*. His work also had an influence on students, as Herbert Moderings demonstrated in his book on Otto Umbehr. Even though Moholy-Nagy had already introduced a more modern approach in 1925, Umbo's photographs still inspired a change in the way students dealt with them.

At that point Meyer was not only open to new approaches in photography, but also in film. He invited the famous Russian director Dsiga Werthoff and the film pioneer Hans Richter to the Bauhaus. In 1929 the Dutch photographer and typographer Piet Zwart gave a month-long course as a guest instructor.

The Goal of Standard Products

Joost Schmidt, cover of the Bauhaus wallpaper catalogue, 1931

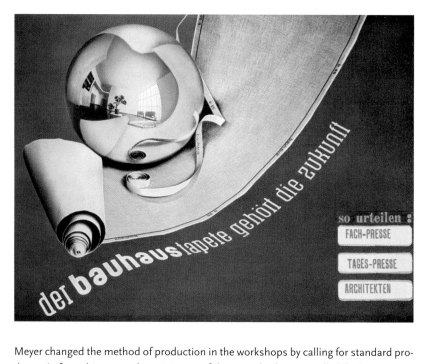

Meyer changed the method of production in the workshops by calling for standard products. At first, this seemed reminiscent of the "standard types" called for by Gropius, however they differed in terms of their theoretical background and practical application. Like Le Corbusier, Meyer also operated on the assumption that there were already many excellent standard products, such as the Thonet line or the light fixtures by Zeiss-Ikon and AEG. In addition, Meyer considered products from the Swiss cooperative movement ideal. In 1924 he created a "co-op" interior, which was documented in photographs as an environment for highly mobile people who did not seek fulfilment in individual extravagancies, but instead were satisfied with proven standard products.

The goal was to develop new standard products in order to make them affordable for a broad cross-section of society. Meyer spoke of a "service to the people". The process of determining needs was to become scientific, instead of "formalistic", which was tantamount to a rejection of Gropius's aesthetics. The cooperation between the metal workshop and the lighting industry was responsible for a number of successes. Production focused on a few prototypes that were manufactured in large numbers. The furniture workshop developed a system of easy assembly, designed a standard *Volkswohnung* (people's home) and furniture for the students' rooms at the *ADGB-Bundesschule*. Bauhaus wallpaper, available in designs to which all of the students contributed, was the most commercially successful product to come out of the Bauhaus workshops. A new sense of aesthetics triumphed, it was manifested in Hannes Meyer's "demonstration charts" which presented objective information in an attractive form.

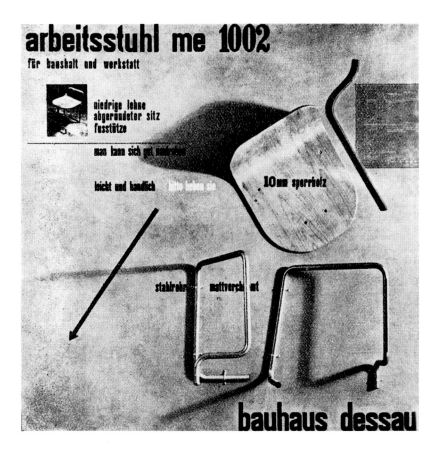

arbeitsstuhl me 1002
für haushalt und werkstatt

niedrige lehne
abgerundeter sitz
fusstütze

man kann sich gut anziehen

leicht und handlich   bitte holen sie

10mm sperrholz

stahlrohr   mattverchromt

bauhaus dessau

Although the courses by Klee, Kandinsky and Albers continued to be offered, all orientation on primary colours, basic forms, and the pictorial and design language developed
by Bayer, Breuer, and Moholy-Nagy was discouraged. Some of the students created
designs for leftist political propaganda or photographed motifs on the fringes of society. In 1928, students in the stage course began criticising the lack of social relevance
of the part of the workshop's director; Schlemmer was responsible for creating the
Bauhaus dances, which were based on space, form, and gesture. They ultimately did
succeed in staging timely pieces that they had choreographed themselves.

The Trade Union School in Bernau, 1928–1930

Left page:

Hannes Meyer, the Trade Union School in Bernau, 1928–1930
A view down the glass corridor on the northwest side of the building. Photo by Walter Peterhans

The entrance is located under the protective canopy roof on the left.
Photo from an advertising folder, 1931

Interior of a student's room
Photo from an advertising folder, 1931

Shortly after the change of directors, at the end of April 1928, Meyer/Wittwer were commissioned to build a school for the ADGB (General Federation of German Trade Unions), where union officials would attend four-week training sessions. Hence the school had to provide housing as well as dining and sports facilities for roughly 130 people. As is the case with Gropius's Bauhaus building, Hannes Meyer's *Bundesschule* can only be understood in total when viewed from the air. Individual, clearly distinguished structures are nestled into the flat landscape of the Mark Brandenburg in the form of a Z, one next to the other. In the long vertical axis, which opens onto a lake to the south-west, there were 60 rooms, for two students each, in four, staggered, three-storey buildings. Meyer based his plan on Pestalozzi's principle of "small groups" and divided the 120 students into twelve groups of ten, for which there were five rooms along each corridor. There is a glass passageway on the north side of the building, which leads in a north-easterly direction to the classrooms, library and gymnasium, set at a 90° angle to the dormitories. Access to the assembly hall, the dining hall and a terrace in the form of a quarter circle opening onto the lake is from the northwest. The drive leading up to the building is from the southwest, where four teacher's houses, partially supported by pylons, are also set at a 90° angle to the rest. The broad, single-storey entrance hall has three symmetrically arranged chimneys from the oil heating plant rising up above it.

Meyer explained in *bauhaus* that the structure of the school building had practically evolved on its own. A number of diagrams illustrate the fact that almost every detail of

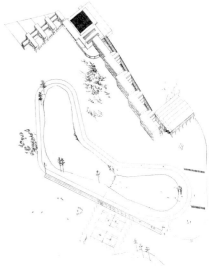

Upper left:
Courtyard with tables and chairs
Photo from an advertising folder 1931

Lower left:
**View of the teachers' houses from the
southeast**
Photo from an advertising folder, 1931

Right:
Plan of the grounds

the design was determined scientifically and that a "relaxed" approach was the human as well as the architectural principle. Meyer wanted this building to negate composition completely, but in fact the clearly delineated building structures are aligned with each other as in New Architecture. Using three chimneys in the design, Meyer added emphasis to the entrance even though it was not located at the centre, but rather to the left. To the right of the entrance he installed a transport ramp with a crane, thereby further playing down the importance of the entrance. Winfried Nerdinger interpreted the school as a "masterpiece of 'poetic functionalism'" and viewed Meyer's architecture as the objective counterpart to similar approaches by Le Corbusier, which were intended to unite organisation, symbolic emphasis, function and construction.

Both in the photographs of the school, most of which are by Peterhans, and in the original building there is no sense of immediate aesthetic appeal comparable to that of Gropius's Bauhaus building, which was a sensation because of its glass façade. Gropius created a form accessible to the viewer by virtue of its structural mass. Despite its qualities, Meyer's remote and for the most part unknown "school in the woods" has never become a destination for pilgrimages as the Bauhaus building has.

Providing for the People, not Catering to Luxury

Hannes Meyer, detailed view of the balcony access buildings with neighbours and residents

Left page:
Architecture Department of the Bauhaus Dessau
Renovation of the tourist office in Dessau, 1928

Hannes Meyer, Architecture Department of the Bauhaus Dessau
Balcony access buildings save on stairways, since the flats are accessed via the arcade balconies on the façade.

In establishing architecture as a course of study, Meyer proved quite inept in dealing with personnel. Hans Wittwer and Johan Niegemann left the Bauhaus at odds with him, and Anton Brenner left after only a year because of differences with Ludwig Hilberseimer. Brenner's successor Edvard Heiberg remained only one semester.

The Törten project gave Meyer an opportunity to provide students with the practical experience considered essential. The commission to build five balcony-access housing blocks as part of the extension of the Törten Housing Estate was Meyer's second at the Bauhaus, and his last. Other projects, to which the city had committed itself, were never executed. Meyer considered these housing blocks a "collective project". The architectural department extended the housing estate designed by Gropius to the southeast, in an austere rectangular grid. The design is noteworthy for two reasons: for one, it is proof of the Bauhaus's political commitment, for another, it represents the first application of Hilberseimer's planning principles. The plan drawn in 1930 shows that there were not only one-storey cottages for the "petite bourgeoisie", there were also multifamily balcony-access housing blocks for the "proletariat", in order to ensure a social mix. Hilbersheimer had promoted balcony-access buildings in *bauhaus* magazine in 1929. He calculated that a minimum of 48 square metres of floor space were required for a flat with a living room, master and children's bedroom. He had also already published articles on the building mix, the characteristic L-shaped, low-rise buildings and on the distinction between residential streets and streets for through traffic. The five, three-storey brick buildings that were completed are on an east-west axis in order to ensure as much sun as possible. Balcony-access buildings require only one staircase to access an entire block of flats with 18 units measuring 47 square metres each. The balcony-access housing blocks were free of the flaws found in the neighbouring Gropius houses, and the residents accepted them then, as they do today.

A classic example of Meyer's approach to design can be found in a note on one of his student's preliminary studies: "the floor plan is calculated on the basis of the following factors". The claim that a solution to any given building task could be found automatically simply by determining the "soft factors" was one that Meyer often repeated. Discussions of aesthetic questions were considered taboo. Technical and functional exercises, like the calculation of the angle of the sunlight, were part of the training in fundamentals.

Hilberseimer taught his theory in the Seminar for Community and City Planning. He had become well known in professional journals through the numerous articles that he had published since the early twenties. Although he never received a public commission, his methods became highly influential, since many of his students applied his principles of city planning after 1945 in West Germany.

Meyer's Dismissal, 1930

Poster design for exhibition "STEIN, HOLZ, EISEN" ("STONE, TIMBER, IRON"), 1930
Erich Mrozek

In one sense Meyer did preserve Gropius's legacy; he continued to run the school in an anti-academic tradition after 1928. In his brochure *Junge Menschen*, published in 1929, he wrote, "young people! what are you looking for at art academies? come to the bauhaus!" His "Open Letter", published in 1930, still described the alternative as "the academy or the Bauhaus" and emphasised the unique character of the art institution. In order for architects to be taught as Meyer saw fit, they needed practical experience with construction projects, since without it the Bauhaus would not differ from "any other technical university" and, as he wrote to Gropius on 16 February 1927, would then be superfluous.

The latent elitism of the school was something Meyer wanted to do away with. He therefore increased the number of students to almost 200. The Bauhaus was not supposed to select only the most talented, but be open to the "proletariat". "The growing proletarian influence at the institute seems to be in keeping with the times", he wrote in his "Open Letter" of 1930. Meyer's shift away from the bourgeois and avant-garde elitist concept was also evident in other aspects: he planned to cooperate with the leftist publishing house Malik-Verlag and the journal *Stein, Holz, Eisen*, both of which represented publications that were not identified with the avant-garde. As director of the Bauhaus, Meyer failed both in human and in political terms; his conceptual approach suggested a Bauhaus that had left the thin air of the avant-garde in favour of a problem-solving approach closer to reality.

In the end, by 1930 there were more people in positions of power interested in seeing Meyer dismissed than in seeing him retained. Some students found the social-political reorientation that he initiated convincing, but not many of the masters agreed. Albers and Kandinsky, as the last representatives of "art", saw their medium-term positions threatened. Outside the Bauhaus, Dessau's museum director Ludwig Grote, facing increasing animosity himself for exhibiting and purchasing modern art, favoured a non-political Bauhaus. The charge against Meyer was that he had fostered a more political climate at the school by never really prohibiting communist activities. He had thereby given the rightist press an opportunity to criticise Dessau's mayor for leaning toward the left. Hesse, in turn, feared every mention of the Bauhaus in the newspapers, since the coalition he led was losing voters, something attributed to their support for the Bauhaus.

Other reasons for Meyer's dismissal were more difficult to categorise in legal terms, and were only discussed behind closed doors. For one, Meyer had been involved in extramarital relationships, something that had already caused an uproar in 1928, and the second "covert" charge was that he had suffered a loss of authority. Meyer rejected directorial hierarchies and wanted to be a "comrade among comrades". He lacked Walter Gropius's authoritative leadership style, he also lacked the "flexibility and mobility" that Ise Gropius considered one of her husband's "most important characteristics". Meyer had no backing of his own within the "Masters' Council". Nevertheless, approval of the measure to dismiss the old director and install a new

Minimum-sized flats were a topic dealt with in Ludwig Hilberseimer's class.
Illustration from the *bauhaus* magazine 1929, Number 2

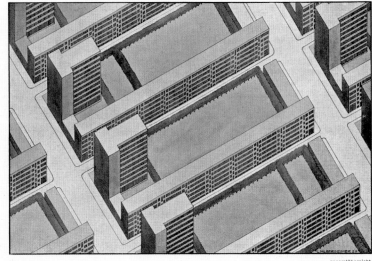

gesamtübersicht

Hannes Meyer goes to the Soviet Union
Cartoon by Adolf Hofmeister, 1930

one, Mies van der Rohe, was only solicited by letter and during school holidays, making it seem like a behind-the-scenes move. Only one critic accused Meyer of not having been radical enough, his press liaison Ernst Kallai who had left him at the end of 1929, drawing the bitter conclusion in the *Weltbühne* the following year that: "His reforms remain a patchwork ... since they run up against the legacy of the previous director— still reflected in the staff, the spirit and the practices of the school—where it cannot be overcome".

Although he was director of the Bauhaus for less than two and a half years, Meyer made a notable impression on some of the students. In the postwar period many of them were inclined to believe that the GDR was the better Germany. Hannes Meyer, who was active on the political left all of his life, wanted to settled in the GDR, after having worked in the USSR, in Mexico and—at the end of his lacklustre career— in Switzerland. However, political intrigue and the animosity of the East Germany government toward the Bauhaus prevented him from doing so. Hannes Meyer died in Switzerland in 1954.

Mies van der Rohe, Director, 1930–1933

Ludwig Hilberseimer and Mies van der Rohe on an excursion to Paretz with other Bauhaus members in May 1933

Why was Mies van der Rohe (1886–1969) chosen? Why did he accept? Mies van der Rohe was one of the leading modern architects in the Weimar Republic and considered non-political. He had been vice-chairman of the *Deutscher Werkbund* since 1926, and commissioned by the organisation to draught a plan for the Weißenhof Exhibition in Stuttgart, where architects from Germany and abroad presented examples of modern residential architecture under his direction. The Stuttgart exhibition was the first large international manifestation of New Architecture in Germany. In 1929 Mies was commissioned to design the German pavilion at the World's Fair in Barcelona, a highly prestigious project.

Mies was born into a family of stonemasons and advanced from the status of craftsman and ornamental draughtsman to that of an architect in just a few years. Like Gropius, he had worked for Peter Behrens (1908–1911). He established himself among the architectural avant-garde after 1923, with designs for a number of high-rises and country houses.

Mies van der Rohe's independent position within the architectural avant-garde and the relationship between material, space, intellect, tradition, and technology that he propagated made him a compelling model for students. Mies declared that architecture must begin with modern industry and technology. In order to recognise its character, however, one ultimately had to make comparisons with the past. Hence, Mies re-introduced history, once rejected by New Architecture, into architecture, something he never explicitly stated.

With these furnishings Mies van der Rohe gave the living room of Gropius's master's house an entirely new look.
Photo by Walter Peterhans, ca. 1931/32

He differentiated between "architecture", which he saw merely as a means to an end, and "the art of building", which he sought to practise. The art of building intended to fulfil "more than just a purpose" according to Mies in 1930. "Standardisation and norms" should not be overestimated, nor social conditions seen as inevitable. By defining these boundaries, Mies distanced himself both from the "formalist" Gropius and the "rationalist" Meyer. Correspondingly, his concept of what needed to be done at the Bauhaus was just as unique. "We are concerned, for the most part, with questions of design posed by the development of technology and industry. I consider dealing with these questions from a cultural point of view to be of utmost importance. It is not a matter of senselessly using new materials; to me it is far more crucial that these materials, which are a given, be used to realise higher spiritual values." His "struggle at the Bauhaus" was dedicated to this end, as he wrote to Martin Mächler in 1933.

Mies steered clear of politics even more clearly than Gropius did. In a statement, from 26 November 1930, characteristic of his leadership at the Bauhaus, he argued that "In order to deal fairly with all political currents, we should not only subscribe to the *Frankfurter Zeitung* [liberal], but also to the *Rote Fahne* [communist] and the *Der Völkische Beobachter* [Nazi]."

In terms of leadership style Mies also differed greatly from Gropius and Meyer. He was described as unapproachable, distant and authoritarian and he tended to adopt a rather elitist attitude.

Ludwig Mies on the grounds of the Berlin Bauhaus, after demonstrating how to lay bricks, 1932

Es ist, wenn kein Wunder geschieht, wieder mal soweit: die Schüler und Schülerinnen des Bauhauses müssen ihre sieben Sachen zusammensuchen und auswandern. Die Schulglocke holt zum letzten Zeichen aus! Die Jungen und Mädel, verbunden durch den Geist produktiver Studienarbeit, müssen sich trennen und auf Wanderschaft gehen. Wohin? Es wird

Vier Etagen Balkone des Atelierhauses

Unterricht in Möbelkonstruktion

Eine Studie auf dem Balkon der Malklasse

ein hoffnungsloser Aufbruch werden — ein Aufbruch ohne Ziel. Als vor Jahren die Gemeinschaft der Bauhaus-Schüler und Bauhaus-Lehrer Weimar verlassen musste, verfolgt von einem zusammengelaufenen Haufen nationalistischer Spiessbürger, war es noch ein Aufbruch mit einem Ziel. Das Ziel hiess Dessau. Heute hat sich in demselben Dessau eine

Aufnahmen A. P.
Alfred Eisenstaedt

DESSAU

Gruppe spiessbürgerlicher Nationalisten zusammengefunden, um die früher freudig begrüssten Emigranten aus Weimar auszutreiben. Mit brutalen Schritten und höhnischem Lachen sind diese Leute in die Bezirke einer freiheitlichen Jugend und eines modernen Studiums eingedrungen. Sie wollen ganze Arbeit machen! Nicht nur die Schüler und Lehrer sollen vertrieben werden — das Schulgebäude soll dem Erdboden gleichgemacht werden. Jungen und Mädchen und Lehrer werden sich in alle vier Winde zerstreuen und vielleicht anderswo lernen und lehren — das Studium des Kunstgewerbes, der Architektur und des Kunsthandwerks aber wird in Deutschland an einer Schule weniger möglich sein: am Bauhaus in Dessau. Wir haben in Deutschland an modernen Kunstgewerbeschulen keinen Ueberfluss. Der Verlust des Bauhauses ist nicht zu verschmerzen.

Zeichenunterricht nach einem beweglichen Modell

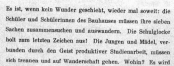

Political Tensions

The collage by the Japanese Bauhaus student Iwao Yamawaki was created to commemorate the closure of the Bauhaus in Dessau in 1932.

Left page:
In 1932 the newspaper "Berliner Tageblatt" reported on the closing of the Dessau Bauhaus.

As director of the Bauhaus he found himself confronted with numerous problems, some of which resulted from the Great Depression of 1929, and some from the increasing antagonism toward the Bauhaus in Dessau. The city reduced its financial support for the Bauhaus markedly. The funding for 1931 and 1932 was notably lower than the expenditures with which Mies reckoned. The kind of public building commissions that Gropius and Meyer had received were no longer available. Space had to be made in the Bauhaus building for the a technical training school, unrelated to the Bauhaus, which had over 1400 students and was expanding rapidly, while the Bauhaus had only 170. The studio flats on three floors of the Preller Building had been turned into workshop space, so that only one floor with a total of seven studios was still available to the Bauhaus.

The intellectual climate at the Bauhaus was still influenced by communist students who had formed the so-called "Kostufra" (Communist Student Faction). The last issue of their journal entitled bauhaus was published in 1932 at the Bauhaus Berlin, indicating how long-lived such ideas were within the student body. They criticised the Bauhaus' participation in the "bourgeois" 1931 Building Exhibition, rather than in the Proletarian Building Exhibition staged as a counter-event. Right wing students also formed an organisation: they made a public appearance when the school was being closed in 1933, petitioning the political authorities to re-open the school. With a series of lectures by speakers such as the philosophers Helmuth Plessner and Hans Freyer addressing the question of anthropological constants in the human race, Mies underlined his new intellectual orientation at the Bauhaus. Another source of aesthetic influence on the Bauhaus was the *Arbeiter-Illustrierte-Zeitung* (AIZ), which featured montages by John Heartfield that inspired the work of Bauhaus students. The famous collage by the Japanese student Iwao Yamawaki "The End of the Dessau Bauhaus", commemorating the school's closure in 1932, was a montage that included photographs from the AIZ.

New Structures

Ludwig Mies van der Rohe, The Home of Today
Berlin Building Exhibition Berlin 1931, the
exhibition house designed by Mies van der Rohe
with Lily Reich's one-storey house (not visible)
behind it

**View of the living room from the dining area in
the exhibition house by Mies van der Rohe at
the Berlin Building Exhibition in Berlin, 1931**

Mies defined the Bauhaus on the basis of architecture, while Gropius had declared
architecture to be the "final goal" on a long path. Consequently, Mies pursued a concept of the Bauhaus that was, for the most part, contrary to Gropius's.

This sort of a Bauhaus required students to be trained in the crafts, since Mies's
"spatial works of art" involved carefully selecting, working with and combining materials. Since the workshops were no long responsible for training apprentices, they could
devote more attention to questions of design, in keeping with Mies's interests. The
courses of study that were introduced in 1927 became well established and remained
in the curriculum even after the Bauhaus relocated to Berlin in 1933, yet at the same
time they continued to change in keeping both with Mies's concepts and the possibilities that still existed in terms of financing and staffing.

In restructuring, Mies had to come to terms with the existing courses on offer and
the teachers who conducted them. The resignation of the director of the textile workshop Gunta Stölzl, in 1931, provided Mies with an opportunity. He named his private
and professional partner Lilly Reich as Stölzl's successor and also put her in charge of
the Interior Decorating Department at the same time. The first and last collection of
three textile albums, produced under Reich's direction, shows how quickly the workshop was able to adapt to the "new spatial limitations". When the school relocated to
Berlin in 1932, Mies considered not rehiring two of the masters, Josef Albers and
Wassily Kandinsky, but then did after all, whereas two other long-standing Bauhaus
masters, Joost Schmidt (advertising) and Alfred Arndt (Interior Design), were not
offered new contracts.

Lilly Reich, Ludwig Hilberseimer (left), and students at Bauhaus, Berlin, April 12, 1933

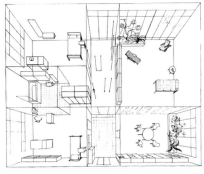

Alfred Arndt, Wilhelm Jakob Hess: possibilities of using combinable furniture in a free-standing single-family house.
This sort of division into small units was contrary to Mies's concept of space.

The collaboration with the two instructors hired by Meyer, Hilberseimer, and Peterhans was so successful that Mies van der Rohe worked with them again when developing his courses in the United States. Mies's friendship with Ludwig Hilberseimer dated back to the early 1920s. In his short term in office he established a basis for a new Bauhaus, the contours of which could be recognised, although it was never programmatically defined in a public context.

Architectural Training under Mies van der Rohe

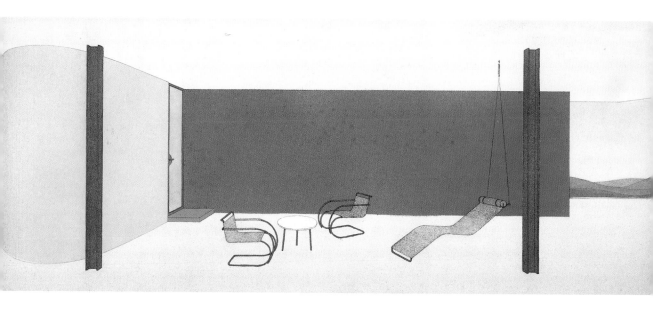

Mies van der Rohe's class
Eduard Ludwig, view of an interior in perspective, 1932

The architectural course, which Mies reduced to six semesters, turned out to be the most attractive programme of study, one in which the classes offered by Mies and Hilberseimer complemented each other. Hilberseimer developed a standard-type, L-shaped house in 1928/29 along with Hugo Häring, which was then dealt with as a single-family house and as a city-planning task. Terence Riley interpreted the task of designing a single-family house, the kind often found within the context of a housing estate, i.e. the smallest building block of a city, as Mies's answer to students' criticism of his "socially irresponsible" commissions. Behind it stood Mies's conviction that only someone able to design a perfect house would be up to more difficult commissions. Quite unlike Meyer, who placed the greatest value on practical building experience, these tasks were only solved on the basis of designs. The details had to be drawn with the greatest care. The open floor plans linked interior and exterior spaces, hence the small single-family houses were located on large parcels of land.

For the students under Meyer, the development of a functional floor plan was the most essential task. Mies taught that there was yet another step to be taken after the purpose has been fulfilled. For example, there should be enough space and light to serve the purpose, but the quality of their design should also provide a new dimension of aesthetic experience. Ludwig Hilberseimer extended the systematic instruction in urban planning, which he had already been offered under Meyer. One of the most elaborate projects was the planning of an ideal solution on the basis of actual conditions for workers in Dessau, the Fichtenbreite Housing Estate, which Hilberseimer and Mies supervised and which later became the topic of a number of theses. Six participants in the original "city planning collective" were members of the

Mies van der Rohe correcting papers
From the left: Annemarie Wilke, Heinrich Neuy, Mies, Werner Klumpp

German Communist Party. Reinhold Rossig received his diploma for a design of a socialist city.

After his emigration to the United States in 1938, Mies developed a curriculum for architecture at Chicago's Armour (later Illinois) Institute of Technology. His reputation as a teacher was, however, soon overshadowed by his fame as a practising architect. To this day, Mies van der Rohe is seen as one of the most influential architects of the twentieth century. He died in 1969.

Information sheet on the "Plate-Light" designed by Heinrich Siegfried Bormann in 1931
The light shines down and is reflected upward.

Reform und Avant-Garde under Mies van der Rohe

Mies van der Rohe's class
Heinrich Bormann, interior of the CEPH House, 1933

"In Germany the struggle against the rationalists will be more difficult than against the academics", Mies van der Rohe wrote to Le Corbusier in 1929. This is a clear indication of Mies's anti-academic attitude, one he was destined to be expressed at the Bauhaus. The number of courses at the Bauhaus was, in comparison to traditional colleges and universities, limited since students at the upper level could not choose between different departments, but only between Mies van der Rohe and Hilberseimer. Students who had transferred from other technical universities to the Bauhaus were nevertheless enthusiastic: in 1932 Hans Kessler, who had studied architecture for four semesters at the Technical University in Stuttgart, praised the small classes that differed greatly from "mass instruction at the university". There were no "senile university professors" at the Bauhaus, here it was "possible to combine everything".

In a discussion with the National Socialist functionary Alfred Rosenberg, Mies described his position in 1933 in a similar manner: "Altogether I have roughly thirty young people in three different semesters, so that I can really work with every single one of them". By "making the course of study shorter", he intended to "increase the course's intensity" thereby offering an alternative concept to the practice at traditional technical universities, where there were "too many specialised disciplines". Criticising the way Mies ran the Bauhaus as "academic", a charge often found in more recent stu-

Architecture class outdoors, on the right the
teacher Alcar Rudelt, ca. 1929–1931

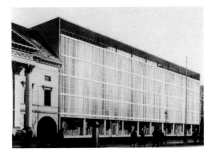

Eduard Ludwig, proposal for renovating the
Borchardt building in Dessau, 1931

dies, does not do justice to his concept of the school. Approaches oriented toward reform and avant-garde elitism overlapped. The number of students was limited to an average of 150 for reasons "of space". Journeymen and applicants who hadn't sat for qualifying examinations could still be accepted and often were. Mies's opinion was that "One should let everyone, who has the wherewithal to build, do so, without considering background or education". Open access and elitism were not contradictions. In the Weimar Republic journeymen were allowed to study architecture at the building trades schools and at some of the academies, but not at technical universities, which for the most part required that students had passed a qualifying examination.

Under Mies the school recovered a sense of its own value, similar to what had evolved at the Weimar Bauhaus. When the small staff voted in favour of the school's dissolution at their final meeting on 20 July 1933, they confirmed their "moral copyright" on the Bauhaus, in the same way the school had done when resignations were submitted in Weimar in 1924.

The Nazi Campaign against the Bauhaus

In 1932 the Bauhaus was still primarily associated with Walter Gropius.
This "obituary" for the Dessau Bauhaus was published in the *Neue Leipziger Zeitung*, 1932

Only a few months after the establishment of the Bauhaus in 1919, the division of the Weimar Republic into a conservative German Nationalist front and a Social Democratic and Communist front was reflected in the struggles surrounding the state-financed school in Weimar. Staffing decisions that had once been purely artistic now became political. The claims staked out by political groups in the cultural arena often reflected a growing polarisation: tradition versus modernism was equal to the Right versus the Left. The Bauhaus was associated with leftist political forces. The closure of the school in Weimar was therefore inevitable when, in spring 1924, a right-wing coalition replaced the formerly leftist government of the Free State of Thuringia. The new government passed a fifty-percent cut in the budget of the despised institution as its first measure.

In the state of Anhalt and in Dessau, where the school relocated in 1925, political conditions remained more favourable for the Bauhaus until 1932. The political climate began to change, however, in 1929 as the Nazi Party grew in strength. They repeated the charge of "cultural Bolshevism", which had dogged the Bauhaus since the Weimar period, calling it a prime example. The Dessau Nazi faction succeeded in having the school closed by communal ordinance in September 1932. Animosities rooted in local politics, and more widespread developments in terms of cultural policy overlapped in this case.

After their enormous election gains in 1932, the National Socialists dominated the discussion on cultural politics, influencing even supporters of the Bauhaus by their accusations. Not only Gropius, but also the museum director Ludwig Grote, Dessau's mayor Fritz Hesse, and architectural critics like Bruno E. Werner attempted to develop arguments to prove that modern tendencies, the Bauhaus among them, were not culturally bolshevist, but German. Mies van der Rohe reopened the Bauhaus as a private institute in Berlin in October 1932, but it only survived for a few months. After the "seizure of power" on 31 January 1933, all cultural institutions were forced to align themselves with Nazi policy.

There were a number of factors that led the teaching staff to vote to disband the Bauhaus shortly after the Nazis had shut it down on 11 April 1933. Open letters and tactical manoeuvring had been to no avail. The city of Dessau had stopped the promised payment of salaries, in breech of contract, and fees for licenses were no longer remitted.

Otti Berger in the cafeteria of the Bauhaus
Dessau on the day of the closure 1932
Photo by Getrud Arndt

Students moving into the Bauhaus Berlin, in
October 1932

Epilogue: The Bauhaus Legend

In 1930 Walter Gropius designed the section of the *Deutscher Werkbund* in Paris.
The photo shows the common room.
·

By the time the Bauhaus was closed in 1933, the term "Bauhaus Style" had become an accepted term in German newspapers and professional journals. The opening of the Bauhaus building in 1926 heightened the public's interest even further. Gropius provided exclusive photographs to the architectural journal *Bauwelt* and to the popular magazine *Das illustrierte Blatt*. In doing so he catered to both professional circles and the wide readership of the newly emerging illustrated magazines. From the moment the Bauhaus had been founded, Gropius had operated on the principle that photos are news.

Hannes Meyer and Mies van der Rohe found themselves caught up in the wake of the public expectations that Gropius had cultivated through his constant presence in the media. Each of them reacted differently. Meyer and Gropius had become secret rivals early on. Meyer wanted to change the Bauhaus in keeping with his leftist politics. In 1928 he hired Ernst Kallai as editor of the magazine *bauhaus* , which immediately ran twice as many pages. In 1929/30 he organised the exhibition "10 Years of the Bauhaus" which, rather than reviewing the history, only presented products from the period in which he was director. His travelling exhibit was, however, eclipsed by the Paris Exhibition of 1930, commissioned by the *Deutscher Werkbund*, organised by Gropius, along with Moholy-Nagy, Breuer and Bayer, as a kind of Bauhaus exhibition.

Bauhaus wallpaper and the Bauhaus lamps produced by Kandem probably made more of an impression on the public than Meyer's public relations work did. An extensive publication, which he had planned for August 1930, never went into print. It is only in his "Open Letter", in the left-liberal magazine *Tagebuch*, that he proved himself equal to Gropius in terms of handling the media. Meyer discussed his dismissal and accused Gropius of having pulled strings behind the scenes. Some of his ironically formulated criticism has become part of the Bauhaus literature. Ultimately, Meyer's attempt to transform the public's image of the Bauhaus, as it had been defined by Gropius, failed because he wavered sporadically between attack, rivalry and denial.

In contrast to Meyer, Mies van der Rohe avoided competing with Gropius in public. He considered "the propagandistic approach of the Bauhaus in the early years to be just what was wrong" and "therefore avoided all propaganda", he wrote to Martin Mächler on 10 May 1933. Under Mies only three, thin issues of the magazine *bauhaus*, which Meyer had used extensively, were ever published, and only one issue contained four lines of text by the new director. There is no coverage of the participation in the big Berlin Building Exhibition of 1931, at which Mies van der Rohe was the curator of the section *Die Wohnung unserer Zeit* (The Modern Home), in which the Bauhaus presented interior furnishings. The extensive commission to furnish Philip Johnson's New York apartment was also never mentioned.

Walter Gropius continued to look upon the Bauhaus as his creation even after 1928, and he worked ceaselessly to make it famous, in the end all over the world. In 1929 the Bauhaus book *von material zu architektur* was published, followed a year later by *bauhausbauten dessau* which Meyer considered an affront, since in it he had no place in the public eye.

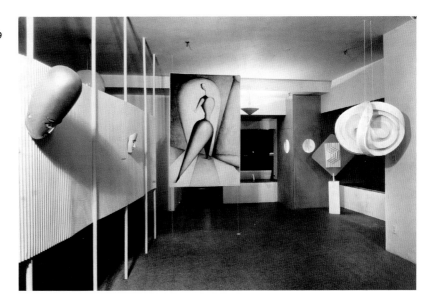

Gropius, who was in great demand at home and abroad as a speaker, began to mention the Bauhaus in his lectures in 1932. In doing so he took an important step in ensuring that the Bauhaus remained a current topic. He freed it of history and nationality. After that Gropius advanced the opinion that he had created a universally valid, and timeless pedagogical model with the Bauhaus, a "common denominator" of design. Gropius thereby took up a topos of the avant-garde—from which the Bauhaus staff in Weimar had drawn a sense of legitimation—the belief that their teaching provided insights that were independent of history and tradition.

On the other hand, Mies van der Rohe, after going to the United States in 1938, almost never talked about the Bauhaus, and when he did so, it was only grudgingly. He left its canonisation up to Walter Gropius. In her publication *Call for action. Mitglieder des Bauhauses in Nordamerika* (Call for Action! Members of the Bauhaus in North America), Grawe interpreted Mies van der Rohe's silence as a "distribution of roles" in which Mies surrendered the historical fame of the Bauhaus to Gropius, while Gropius conceded the role of a successful American architect to him.

Gropius's "Reinterpretation of the Bauhaus" reduced it to an idea that is often referred to als legendary. Yet we must bear in mind that this legend was constructed by Gropius. He ensured that "his" Bauhaus was reflected in the media and, although it has been the subject of a number of critical studies, this image of the Bauhaus has lost none of its iconographic power. It is thus now imperative that the history of the Bauhaus be written with as critical eye on Walter Gropius.

Bibliography

▶ Balg, Ilse, ed. Martin Mächler, Weltstadt Berlin. Schriften und Materialien. Berlin: Galerie Wannsee Verlag, 1986.
▶ Bauhaus-Archiv Berlin. Der vorbildliche Architekt. Mies van der Rohes Architekturunterricht 1930–1958 am Bauhaus und in Chicago. Berlin: Nicolaische Verlagsbuchhandlung Beuermann GmbH, 1986.
▶ Grawe, Gabriele Diana. Call for Action. Mitglieder des Bauhauses in Nordamerika. Weimar: Verlag und Datenbank für Geisteswissenschaften, 2002.
▶ Hahn, Peter, ed. bauhaus berlin. Auflösung Dessau, 1932 Schließung Berlin 1933, Bauhäusler und Drittes Reich. Weingarten: Kunstverlag Weingarten, 1985.
▶ Hüter, Karl-Heinz. Das Bauhaus in Weimar. Studie zur gesellschaftspolitischen Geschichte einer deutschen Kunstschule. Berlin: Akademie-Verlag, 1976.
▶ Jaeggi, Annemarie: Adolf Meyer. Der zweite Mann. Ein Architekt im Schatten von Walter Gropius. Argon Verlag, Berlin, 1994
▶ Meyer, Hannes. "Mein Hinauswurf aus dem Bauhaus. Offener Brief an Herrn Oberbürgermeister Hesse, Dessau, 1930". In Meyer-Bergner, Lena. Hannes Meyer. Bauen und Gesellschaft, pp. 67–73. Dresden: Verlag der Kunst, 1980.
▶ Möller, Werner and Wolfgang Thöner. "Das Bauhaus – Eine Balance in mehreren Akten". In Bauhaus, Dessau, Chicago, New York, edited by Georg W. Költzsch and Margarita Tupitsyn, pp. 14–19. Cologne: Dumont Verlag, 2000.
▶ Nerdinger, Winfried. Walter Gropius. Berlin: Gebr. Mann, 1985.
▶ Nerdinger, Winfried. "Anstößiges Rot. Hannes Meyer und der linke Baufunktionalismus – ein verdrängtes Kapitel der Architekturgeschichte". In Hannes Meyer, 1889–1954 Architekt, Urbanist, Lehrer, pp.12–29. Berlin: Ernst und Sohn, 1989.
▶ Nerdinger, Winfried. "Das Bauhaus zwischen Mythisierung und Kritik". In: Die Bauhaus-Debatte 1953, edited by U. Conrads, M. Droste, W. Nerdinger und H. Strohl, pp. 7–19. Braunschweig/Wiesbaden: Vieweg & Sohn, 1994.
▶ Pommer, Richard. "Mies van der Rohe and the Political Ideology of the Modern Movement". In Critical Essays, edited by Franz Schulze, pp. 96–145. Cambridge, Mass.: MIT Press, 1989.
▶ Spaeth, David, ed. Dearstyne, Howard: Inside the Bauhaus. New York: Rizzoli, 1986
▶ Wahl, Volker. Die Meisterratsprotokolle des Staatlichen Bauhauses Weimar 1919–1925, compiled by Ute Ackermann. Weimar: Verlag Hermann Böhlau, Nachfolger, 2001.

For further information see:
▶ Wingler, Hans Maria. Das Bauhaus Weimar Dessau Berlin 1919–1933. Bramsche: Verlag Gebr. Rasch & Co. and M. DuMont Schauberg, 3rd ed. 1975.

Credits

Acknowledgement

Many thanks to Winfried Nerdinger for his help and criticism.

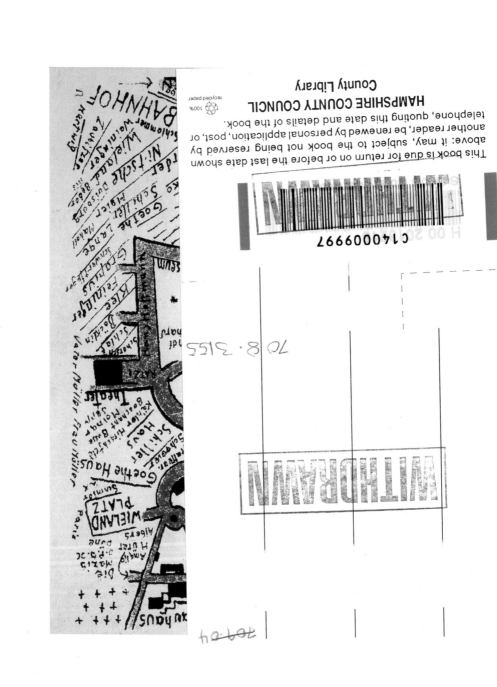